Reading Shakespeare Today

# OTHELLO

Edith Jones and Tatiana Ryckman

Cavendish Square
New York

Published in 2017 by Cavendish Square Publishing, LLC
243 5th Avenue, Suite 136, New York, NY 10016



First Edition



Library of Congress Ca-taloging-in-Publication Data

Names: Jones, Edith, author. Ryckman, Tatiana, author.
Title: Othello / Edith Jones and Tatiana Ryckman.
Description: New York : Cavendish Square, 2017. |
Series: Reading Shakespeare today | Includes index.
Identifiers: ISBN 9781502623331 (library bound) | ISBN 9781502623348 (ebook)
Subjects: LCSH: Shakespeare, William, 1564-1616. Othello--Juvenile literature.
Classification: LCC PR2829.J66 2017 | DDC 822.3'3--dc23

Editorial Director: David McNamara
Editor: Caitlyn Miller
Copy Editor: Rebecca Rohan
Associate Art Director: Amy Greenan
Designer: Lindsey Auten
Production Coordinator: Karol Szymczuk
Photo Research: J8 Media

The photographs in this book are used by permission and through the courtesy of: Shutterstock.com, front, back cover and background throughout the book; p. 6 kenny1/Shutterstock.com; p. 9 theatrepix/Alamy Stock Photo; p. 13 Collection Christophel/Alamy Stock Photo; p. 16 Work Projects Administration Poster Collection/Library of Congress/File: W.P.A. Federal Theatre Presents "Faustus" by Christopher Marlowe LCCN00650238.tif/Wikimedia Commons (Public Domain); p. 28 Leemage/Universal Images Group/Getty Images; p.30 Ann Ronan Pictures/Print Collector/Hulton Archive/Getty Images; p. 34 Francois Bouchot/Getty Images; pp. 37, 50 AF archive/Alamy Stock Photo; p. 39 Sotheby's (http://www.sothebys.com/en/auctions/ecatalogue/2008/old-master-and-19th -century-european-art-n08406/lot.254.html) image (http://www.sothebys.com/conten t/dam/stb/lots/N08/N08406/N08406-254-lr-1.jpg)/File: John William Waterhouse - Touchstone, The Jester.jpg /Wikimedia Commons/(Public Domain); pp. 41, 43 Geraint Lewis/Alamy Stock Photo; p. 48 De Agostini Picture Library/Getty Images; p. 52 Sammyday (2010-10-23)/File: Théodore Chassériau - Le coucher de Desdémone (1849).jpg/Wikimedia Commons/(Public Domain); p. 54 Private Collection/© Look and Learn/Bridgeman Images; p. 56 Folger Shakespeare Library Digital Image Collection http://luna.folger.edu/luna/servlet/s/g3owdb/William Salter, 1857/File: Othello's Lamentation.jpg/Wikimedia Commons/(CCA/SA 4.0 International); p. 59 Attributed to James Northcote (1746-1831)/ Christie's (http://www.christies.com/lotfinder/lot_details.aspx?intObjectID=5537632)/File: Ira Aldridge (1807-1867), in the character of Othello, Attributed to James Northcote (1746-1831).jpg/Wikimedia Commons (Public Domain); p. 61 MIRAMAX/BASHA, BOB/Album/Newscom; p. 64 Bridgeman Images; p. 66 Apic/Hulton Archive/Getty Images; p. 69 Afro Newspaper/Gado/Archive Photos/Getty Images; p. 81 Print Collector/Getty Images; p. 83 Dorling Kindersley/Getty Images; p. 87 Land of Lost Content/Heritage Images/Hulton Archive/Getty Images; p. 91 Bettina Strenske/Photoshot/Newscom.

Printed in the United States of America

# CONTENTS

## Introduction

# SHAKESPEARE AND HIS WORLD

Even without reading one of William Shakespeare's plays or sonnets, most people are able to quote his famous lines. How can one man's writing be so significant that his name is still synonymous with great literature four hundred years after his death?

Though much of his life is shrouded in mystery, most historians believe Shakespeare was born in England in 1564 to a large family. While in good public standing, his family was constantly struggling to stay out of debt, and many wonder how someone with such an unstable background could become the most revered writer of all time.

From the few records historians have found, it appears Shakespeare began gaining recognition for his playwriting in 1592. His plays started to appear in print in individual, or "quarto," editions in 1594, but none of these bore his name until 1598. Although his tragedies are now ranked as his supreme achievements, his name was first associated with comedies and with plays about English history. Known affectionately as the Bard, Shakespeare became famous for his skill writing humor and human suffering in equal measure.

In his lifetime, plays were produced for commoners as well as royalty, capturing the imagination of the rich and poor alike. This wide appeal meant that Shakespeare was versed in lofty literary references familiar to the educated as well as the trials and joys of the peasants that filled the Globe, his famous London theater.

Because Shakespearean English doesn't sound like modern English, it's easy to imagine he was a stuffy old playwright, but nothing could be farther from the truth. Shakespeare's work is riddled with brazen critiques of cultural norms and irreverent comedy. Shakespeare's own history is something of a mystery, and many historians have speculated on the mischief he may have been involved in. These historical rumors are the premise for modern films, such as 1998's Oscar-winning movie *Shakespeare in Love*.

It is the Bard's accessibility that has allowed him to stand the test of time. His 38 plays and 154 sonnets have been studied and reinterpreted for centuries, and every generation reads their own experience in his texts. Shakespeare's most famous plays include *Romeo and Juliet*, *A Midsummer Night's Dream*, *Hamlet*, and *Othello*, which are considered among the most influential works ever written.

These plays have been performed all over the world and re-created in countless other mediums, including film, television, comics, rap music, and cartoons. Some of the most famous film stars in modern times got their start in theater, performing Shakespeare's famous plays. Modern adaptations of Shakespeare's work include the 1996 film *Romeo and Juliet*, starring Leonardo DiCaprio, and the famous Broadway musical *West Side Story*, which

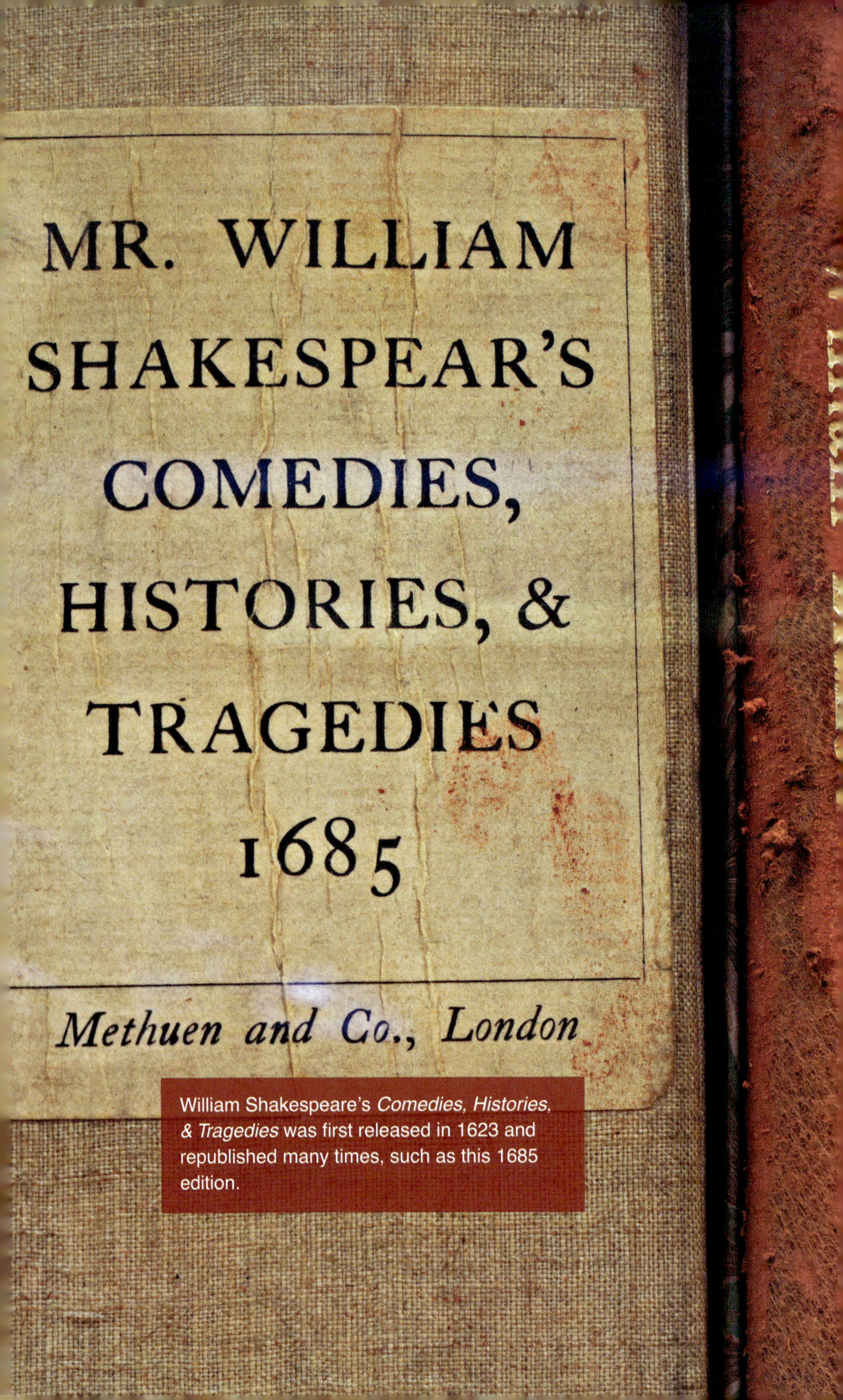


William Shakespeare's *Comedies, Histories, & Tragedies* was first released in 1623 and republished many times, such as this 1685 edition.

is based on the tragic premise of the same play. Julia Stiles starred in a film adaptation of *Othello*, as well as the movie *Ten Things I Hate About You*, which was based on the tragicomedy, *The Taming of the Shrew.*

Many of today's great artists, writers, and musicians still find Shakespeare's work inspiring. Ben Jonson, England's poet laureate in Shakespeare's time, regarded the Bard as the equal of the great classical Greek tragedians Aeschylus, Sophocles, and Euripides, accurately predicting that "He was not of an age, but for all time."

## Chapter One

# Shakespeare and *Othello*

*Othello, the Moor of Venice* feels, in many ways, like the most modern of Shakespeare's tragedies. One contemporary Shakespearean critic has called *Othello* "the tragedy of choice" for the current generation.

But what exactly does that mean? What makes a tragedy more or less relevant to any given generation? Primarily, it conveys the idea that themes once considered minor elements in the drama–issues of race, gender, and class–have become its main concerns for both audiences and critics.

To be sure, Shakespeare took impressive risks in writing *Othello*, in creating both a black protagonist and strong-willed female characters. (Unfortunately, the theater's cast was well behind Shakespeare's vision, and all the roles were filled by white men in his day.) Even today in America, issues of race and gender are pressing cultural and political debates. Many have asked

Issues of race and gender are at the forefront of *Othello*.

if the laws that demand equality for all really ensure that people are treated equally. This dynamic is at the center of *Othello* for modern audiences. While the comments from minor characters on race may not have stood out to Shakespeare's theatergoers, today the same comments might make an audience cringe.

Likewise, the strong female roles written for Desdemona and Emilia are hard to ignore. At a time when women were largely seen as a blank slate upon which men might project their desires or simply as wives and mothers, Shakespeare created these two stubborn women. Desdemona's blind devotion to Othello—even in the face of his violent suspicion—is more of a comment on her strength of character and dedication to principle than on her willingness to be beaten into submission. Even more impressive is Desdemona's brazen display of affection for Othello in front of her father, who is opposed to the interracial marriage. In this way she asserts that she is not *anyone's* property (as women were commonly seen) and will make choices for herself.

Emilia, older and more world-weary than Desdemona, lacks the young woman's undying devotion, but makes up for it with a wealth of ethics. Though she, too, obeys her husband and does not scold him when he makes unattractive comments about women, Shakespeare allows her poignant dialogue in which she challenges societal norms and expectations of women.

## The Foundation of a Play

*Othello* features one of Shakespeare's smallest casts. This narrow focus, especially on the three main characters—the African general Othello; his white Venetian wife,

Desdemona; and his devious ensign Iago—draws both audiences and readers even closer to the tragedy at hand. In fact, one or more of these three characters are on stage for all but one of the play's fifteen scenes.

*Othello*'s limited time frame also intensifies the play's sparse, modern effect. The Bard's other tragedies, including *Hamlet*, *Macbeth*, and *King Lear*, span months—even years—of time. In *Othello,* however, Shakespeare presents only two or three days and nights in the lives of his characters.

The way these characters are represented today surely looks different from performances in Shakespeare's time. As previously mentioned, women were forbidden from performing in the theater, thus all female roles were played by men and boys. The modern portrayal of the lead role—that of Othello, himself—would certainly look strange to theatergoers in Shakespearian times. Though the role is famous as a rare example of a black hero in literature of its time, it was traditionally played by white actors. (While writing a role for a black character was acceptable—just as roles for women were—it would have been radical to actually allow a black man to play the role.)

The theaters were also very different from our modern buildings, with plush seats and elaborate set design. Plays were extremely popular in the Bard's day, but they were primitive, too. They had to be performed outdoors in the afternoon because of the lack of indoor lighting. Often the "theater" was merely an enclosed courtyard. It is likely that the versions of Shakespeare's plays that we know today were not performed in full, but shortened to about two hours for their actual performance.

## *The Bard and the Beast*

WILLIAM SHAKESPEARE'S PLAYS have been adapted for the silver screen countless times, but did you know the Bard frequently makes guest appearances in classic Disney cartoons?

In the classic *Beauty and the Beast*, Belle reads to the Beast from *Romeo and Juliet*, thus beginning their romance. Later in the film, during the riot scene, the evil Gaston quotes a line from Macbeth, "Screw your courage to the sticking place." When, in the movie *Aladdin*, Aladdin asks for his first wish, the Genie quotes Caesar's dying words from the end of *Julius Caesar*, "Et tu, Brute?" *Toy Story 3* has a brief reenactment of *Romeo and Juliet*, complete with the iconic balcony scene.

Jack Skellington, from *Nightmare Before Christmas*, pops his own head off to wax poetic, a short but clear reference to the scene in *Hamlet* where Hamlet holds Yorick's skull. And *The Lion King* is actually based on *Hamlet*–a young prince is haunted by his father's ghost and returns to his kingdom to avenge his father's murder by an evil uncle. It's amazing to see just how many ways Shakespeare's ideas have influenced modern film.

But perhaps no Disney movie has quite as many references to Shakespeare as the sequel to Pocahontas, *Pocahontas II: Journey to a New World.* In this film Shakespeare himself is seen singing among the London commoners. When a skull rolls off a cart carrying the dead, Shakespeare asks in song, "To be or not to be"–suggesting

The balcony scene from *Romeo and Juliet* has been referenced countless times in popular culture, such as in *Toy Story 3.*

the inspiration for his famous play *Hamlet.* Despite the historical inaccuracy—Shakespeare died months before the real Pocahontas arrived in England and had moved back to Stratford-upon-Avon years before—it's hard not to recognize Shakespeare's incredible reach and persistent presence in culture.

Eventually, more regular theaters were built, featuring a raised stage extending into the audience. Poor spectators (illiterate "groundlings") stood on the ground around it, at times exposed to rain and snow. Wealthier people sat in raised tiers above. Aside from some costumes, there were few props or special effects and almost no scenery.

Unlike modern theater, Shakespeare's Globe Theatre—he describes it as "this wooden O"—had no curtain separating the stage from the audience. This allowed intimacy between the players and the spectators.

Today, we sometimes speak of "live entertainment." In Shakespeare's day, of course, all entertainment was live, because recordings, films, television, and radio did not yet exist. Even printed books were a novelty.

Most people were illiterate peasants who lived on farms that they seldom left; cities grew up along waterways and were subject to frequent plagues that could wipe out much of the population within weeks. When plagues struck London, the government might order the theaters to be closed to prevent the spread of disease among crowds. (They remained empty for nearly two years from 1593 to 1594.)

Money—in coin, not paper—was scarce and hardly existed outside the cities. By today's standards, even the rich were poor. Life was precarious. Most children died young, and famine or disease might kill anyone at any time. Everyone was familiar with death. Starvation was not rare or remote, as it is to most of us today. Medical care was poor and might kill as many people as it healed.

This was the grim background of Shakespeare's theater during the reign of Queen Elizabeth I, who ruled from 1558 until her death in 1603. During that

period, England was also torn by religious conflict, often violent, among Roman Catholics who were loyal to the Pope, adherents of the Church of England who were loyal to the queen, and the Puritans, who would take over the country in the revolution of 1642. Under these conditions, entertainment was a luxury out of most people's reach.

Indeed, even the spectators in Shakespeare's day responded differently to his plays than we do today, reacting rowdily to what was happening onstage, not listening in reverent silence. After all, they had come to have fun! Few in the audience were scholars, and a play had to amuse people who could not read. Actors had to be versatile, skilled not only in acting, but also in fencing, singing, dancing, and acrobatics.

It is stunning to think the first performances of the most famous plays in the English language were acted out against this primitive backdrop.

## A Source of Inspiration

Shakespeare's main source for *Othello* was an Italian tale by Giovanni Battista Giraldi (also known as Cinthio). In Giraldi's original work, first published in 1565, a beautiful Venetian woman named Disdemona marries a North African captain referred to only as "the Moor." Because she has previously rejected the Moor's ensign, he convinces the captain that she has been unfaithful and plays on the Moor's unease about his race. Later in Giraldi's story, the Moor and his ensign murder Disdemona; her relatives ultimately avenge her death. As *Othello* reveals, Shakespeare breathed a much deeper life into this melodramatic plot.

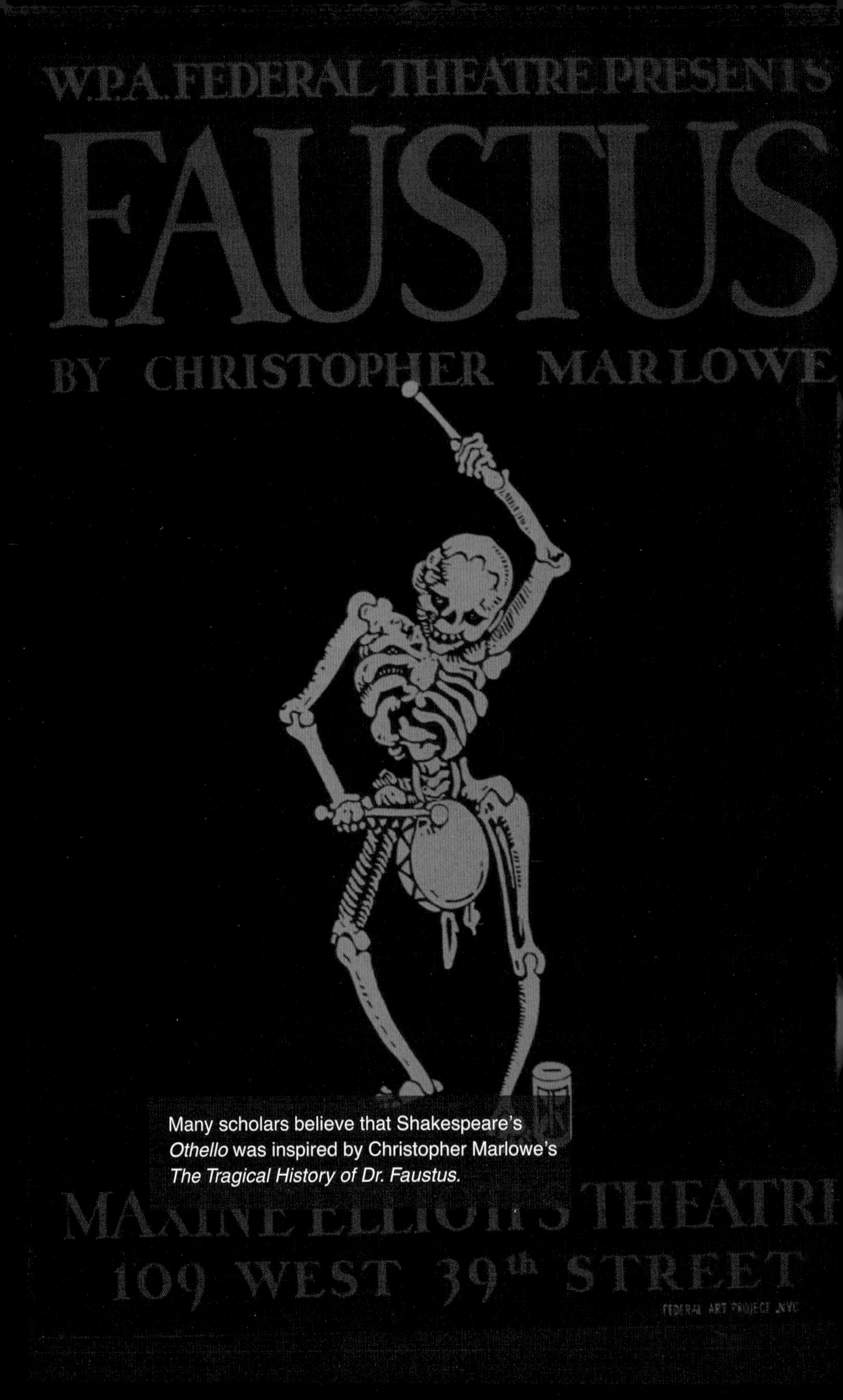


Many scholars believe that Shakespeare's *Othello* was inspired by Christopher Marlowe's *The Tragical History of Dr. Faustus.*

Some scholars have traced the influence of another play, *The Tragical History of Dr. Faustus*, by Shakespeare's contemporary Christopher Marlowe. Written around 1589, *Dr. Faustus* tells the story of a magician who sells his soul to the devil to obtain complete knowledge but ends up with nothing. The closeness between the characters of Othello and Iago seems to parallel that between Faustus and his devil in Marlowe's play.

But then again, there are also plenty of historians who insist that Shakespeare's plays may in fact have been written by Marlowe. In spite of the controversy of authorship, most scholars date the Bard's writing of *Othello* to around 1603–1604. A record exists of the play being performed by the King's Men at Court on November 1, 1604. Two versions of the play's text exist. One is the shorter quarto dated 1622, and the other appears in the great Folio of Shakespeare's plays from 1623. The Folio version is longer, by about 160 lines, and it often serves as the basis for most current editions.

## The Drama Persists

The issue of race continues to spur debate about *Othello* and makes the play ripe for modern interpretations. From the opening scene, the interracial marriage between Othello and Desdemona colors all aspects of the play. Race also provides further motivation for the resentful Iago to destroy the general's happiness. His insults often turn on the relationship between the black Moor and his white wife.

Modern audiences must remember that Elizabethan England had few immigrants or people of color. North African Moors—and in particular those with darker skin—would probably have been feared in Shakespeare's day, especially because many were Muslims. This affected both the way the role was received by the audiences, as well as who could play the role, as mentioned earlier. At times, Shakespeare's characters and their words reflect the stereotypes of his age, yet he manages to make his characters three-dimensional and human. His other plays also contain many racial insults to Jews, Africans, Italians, Irish, and others. Today he would be called "insensitive"; perhaps in none of his plays is this as clear as in *Othello*. Because modern audiences *know* that this insensitivity is wrong, though inequality persists in many aspects of modern culture, Shakespeare's bold tale of discrimination continues to act as a commentary on our world today.

## History Plays Out

Issues about colonialism and the culture clash that often follows have also surfaced in more recent productions. A number of European countries sold African natives into slavery. Although this aspect of colonialism does not appear to be Shakespeare's main concern, Othello does refer to being sold into slavery in his youth. The Venetian colony of Cyprus also serves as a plot device and one of the play's main settings. Shakespeare uses these two settings to draw contrasts between the cultured city-state of Venice and its wilder colony at Cyprus.

In this play, contemporary audiences will savor one of Shakespeare's finest creations, the villainous Iago. In no other play has Shakespeare concentrated evil in such a blatantly wicked character. Whereas the general, Othello, is a man of action, Shakespeare crafts a master of rhetoric and manipulator of language in Iago. Over the centuries, the character has become the prototype for many villains in both literature and film.

*Othello*'s influence is indisputable. The play challenges us to question stereotypes about everything from race to class. Shakespeare's ability to make audiences think and engage with his work is remarkable considering he lived centuries ago. In the next chapter, we'll take a scene-by-scene look at the play.

## Chapter Two

# The Play's the Thing

*Othello* vies with *Hamlet* and *King Lear* as Shakespeare's most supreme tragedy. Its complex roles have been performed by some of the greatest actors the world has ever seen, both on stage and on screen. Orson Welles did a budget European version of the play in 1952, and Laurence Olivier's 1965 film performance is stunning. It has been said that Olivier would only approach the part by honoring, even emulating, Paul Robeson's definitive interpretation that ran on Broadway in 1943. (Robeson was the second black actor to play Othello, the Moor of Venice, and he did so to critical acclaim, though sadly his performance was never filmed.) Maggie Smith plays a formidable Desdemona opposite Olivier, and her youth and energy will surprise younger audiences who know her only from the Harry Potter films or the television show *Downton Abbey*. Laurence Fishburne brilliantly portrayed Othello in the 1995 film, costarring with Kenneth Branagh as a surprisingly human Iago. As recently as 2001, the play has been remade for the screen in the movie *"O"* starring Mekhi Phifer as Odin (a modern, basketball-playing version of Othello), Julia Stiles as Odin's girlfriend (Desdemona), and Josh Hartnett as Hugo, Odin's jealous friend (an updated Iago).

The first time a black man played Othello was at the end of the 1800s. Ira Aldridge was critiqued in *The Times* as having only one advantage over a white actor—that he need not wear makeup. By making this real-world insensitive comment, the reviewer ignored the wealth of experiences Aldridge may have been able to draw on to play the part most successfully. After suggesting the choice to use a black actor would be fine for a small theater but not an establishment of national acclaim, the critic had to admit the show had been well received.

It was not until the 1960s that the complaints of critics reversed, and one such critic complained that it was outrageous to have white men playing the part as a racial stereotype, rather than giving the role its due.

The first instance of a female playing the role of Desdemona was in the 1660s, possibly by the actress Margaret Hughes, who appears in cast lists toward the end of the decade. The English poet, playwright, and actor, Thomas Jordan, wrote an introduction to the audience supporting the leading lady and encouraging the audience to do the same—lest they think her a woman of ill repute for performing in the theater. In a smart turn of phrase Jordan compares the actress's impeccable moral character to that of Desdemona, implying that should the audience choose to question her scruples for acting, they would be making the same fatal mistake as Othello.

The poet went so far as to address the female members of the audience, saying that by begrudging her this role they would be acting against their own interests.

The play has also been rewritten as a libretto for two different operas by Rossini and Verdi, and reimagined in countless iterations through many mediums of art.

So many excellent performers have inhabited these roles and interpreted the characters in their own signature styles, you can readily create your own star cast to act out the drama in your mind as you read Shakespeare's famous text.

## Setting the Stage

Because they are working with different budgets and technology, film and theater adaptations of Othello may not always look alike. Film has the versatility to use the real world as a stage (borrowing an idea from Shakespeare himself: "All the world's a stage, and all the men and women merely players.") The 2001 film, *"O,"* for example, is set in a high school. Rather than being at war, the students play their rivals on the basketball court. This setting is vastly different from Shakespeare's original, primitive theater, and still very different from the set design imagined for today's performances.

Depending on budget, some theaters may use a single prop to represent an entire set—a bed to suggest an entire bedroom, for instance. Other productions may be able to build an elaborate set that changes with each scene, though it's important to remember the more changes that occur throughout a performance, the more people are needed to help change the set each time the stage goes dark.

## Act I, Scene 1

### Overview

*Othello* opens with a night scene as two men, Iago and Roderigo, meet on the streets of Venice. Iago admits his hatred for his general, the Moor Othello, who has made Iago an ensign and given the desired post of lieutenant to another man, Cassio. At the same time Roderigo reveals that he is angry because Othello has run off with Desdemona, a woman who rejected Roderigo's earlier advances.

Iago suggests that they wake Desdemona's father, the Venetian senator Brabantio, and tell him that his daughter has eloped with the black Moor. An appalled Brabantio vows to rouse the Duke of Venice and get a band of armed men to find Desdemona and Othello.

### Analysis

Shakespeare immediately establishes Iago as a master of persuasion who is filled with hatred for Othello. In his first long speech, Iago delivers a tirade about losing the position of lieutenant and his belief that he was more suited for the position than Cassio. Iago's repeated use of the term "the Moor" to describe Othello indicates his awareness of Othello's skin color, and Iago also openly admits to being a dissembler, one who feels one way but intentionally acts another. As he tells Roderigo: "I am not what I am."

Through the dialogue, Shakespeare quickly establishes the power of Iago's manipulation. Both Iago and Roderigo discuss their envious feelings–Iago for Cassio and Roderigo for Othello. Through that envy, Shakespeare lays the foundation for Iago's plotting and for the play's tragedy.

Roderigo responds positively to Iago's anger for Othello and hatred for Cassio, and he readily accepts the ensign's advice. With Iago prompting Roderigo to cause a ruckus when he awakens Brabantio, the two men set out to expose Desdemona's marriage to Othello. At first Brabantio believes Roderigo is still hurting from Desdemona's rejection, but Roderigo persuades the senator that Othello has seduced his daughter.

Shakespeare also uses the scene to inform us of the play's war plot: The Venetians have been fighting the Turks in an ongoing war over the Venetian colony at Cyprus.

## Act I, Scene 2

### Overview

Later in the night, Iago and Othello meet in front of the Moor's lodgings. Iago claims that he has killed men in war, but he would never plot to murder someone–or else he would have killed Brabantio for speaking so rudely about Othello. He then tells Othello that he is worried about the influence Brabantio may have on the Duke of Venice.

Othello defends his own reputation, his royal background, and his long service to Venice. He also insists that he truly loves Desdemona, or he would never have risked such a negative reaction.

Othello's new lieutenant Cassio arrives, bringing orders that the Moor is to meet with the duke and other senators who have called an emergency session to deal with the conflict in Cyprus. Just as Iago is about to tell Cassio about the general's marriage, Othello returns with Brabantio and Roderigo, along with others who are carrying torches and weapons. Brabantio and Roderigo's mob has taken up arms against Othello. Swords are drawn, but Othello manages to calm everyone down.

Brabantio then accuses Othello of using magic to seduce Desdemona. Othello convinces Brabantio—who wants to have him arrested—to accompany him to the Senate, where the old senator can then formally accuse Othello of being a "foul thief."

Hearing that the duke has summoned Othello in the middle of the night, a surprised Brabantio agrees to plead his case in front of the Venetian Senate.

## Analysis

On the heels of the previous scene, in which Iago openly expressed his hatred for Othello, his audacity becomes all too clear in his syrupy words of loyalty to the Moor's "honor." The embittered ensign presents himself as a man of "conscience" who would gladly kill for his general. This is a strong reference to the mythological Janus, a Roman god with two faces.

Othello's first speech is a rousing defense of his own character: he feels confident that he can rely on his reputation and accomplishments to persuade Brabantio. He also refers to his royal upbringing and insists that he is equal in bearing to Desdemona's family.

Cassio's arrival and summons reinforce Othello's importance in Venice. He has been "hotly called for" by the Duke, who is apparently concerned with the developing military events in Cyprus.

# Othello *Goes Digital*

IT'S EASY TO tweet @Shakespeare, or to "like" his latest posts on Facebook. On nearly every social media platform Shakespeare awaits, and the anonymous users behind his name post famous lines, the latest news about performances of his plays, or even new rumors about his life. Though his characters are a little less conspicuous–and enjoy thousands fewer followers–they're still out there, often fully inhabiting their roles online just as they would on the stage.

You can find Othello reacting to the events of the fateful few days covered in the play on Twitter, posting under the handle @OthellotheBeast. The posts are themselves a performance, and some are ominous, hinting at the turmoil filling the character's soul. For example, just before his threat, "Say your prayers Desdemona ..." he posts a single hashtag: #imdoingthisforlove.

A video on YouTube titled "Othello Project Social Media Manipulation" is actually a reenactment of the first act of the *Othello* story from Iago's perspective. The action plays out via private messages and status updates on Facebook. We hear Iago's sarcastic and bitter thoughts narrated as he moves between private messages, cursing his general, Othello, to his friend Roderigo, then a moment later praising Othello's choice of lieutenant in a conversation with his superior. When he sees Desdemona's status update, "feeling loved," it seems Iago may truly become ill.

And what about the ladies of *Othello*? Desdemona can be found blogging about her arrival in Cyprus, and a band by the name of Desdemona y Othello can be streamed from Myspace. A handful of Emilias can be found on Facebook with the name Emilia Othello; one of the profiles for this character has just one update, a line that's sad given the well-known ending to the play: "Hoping for the best."

The mythical god Janus is known for being “two-faced,” an apt comparison to the villainous Iago.

Brabantio's accusation that Othello has used "chains of magic" and "foul charms" to lure Desdemona to him reflects his disparaging view of Othello's race—or as he calls him: "such a thing as thou." These remarks also emphasize the view that the African Othello is exotic and must therefore be a practitioner of evil arts.

# Act I, Scene 3

## Overview

In the chamber of the Venetian Senate, the duke and his senators discuss different reports of the movement of the Turkish fleet and conclude that its target is the island of Cyprus. The duke decides to send Othello to take over command of the Venetian defenders, who are presently under the guidance of the less-experienced Montano.

Othello and Brabantio, along with their separate supporters, arrive to discuss the conflict over Desdemona. The duke asks for evidence of Brabantio's claims that Othello has bewitched the old man's daughter. Othello suggests that they send for Desdemona so she can explain the truth, and then he offers a full account of his courtship.

Once Desdemona arrives, she confirms Othello's account of their relationship in front of her father and the senators and thereby vindicates the Moor. The duke accepts the explanation and then commissions Othello to proceed to Cyprus. Desdemona asks if she may accompany Othello on his mission. The duke agrees, and Othello assigns the duty of transporting his wife to Iago, whom he describes as "a man ... of honesty and trust."

Unhappy with the outcome of his plea, Brabantio leaves with a parting warning to Othello about Desdemona's

This nineteenth-century print shows Desdemona's father, Brabantio, agreeing to let her marry Othello.

deceptive nature: "She has deceived her father," he advises, "and may thee."

Once all others leave, Roderigo tells Iago that he will drown himself with grief over losing Desdemona. Assuring Roderigo that Desdemona will grow tired of Othello, Iago then convinces him to get some money and follow Desdemona to Cyprus and to use a beard to disguise himself. Roderigo exits, asserting that he will sell all his land to acquire the necessary funds.

Left alone onstage, Iago derides Roderigo as a "fool," easily parted from his money, someone whom Iago can use for "sport and profit." He reiterates his hatred for Othello and concocts his plan to steal Cassio's place as lieutenant by convincing Othello that Cassio has been "too familiar" with Desdemona.

## Analysis

Shakespeare masterfully moves the action from scene to scene in Act I. In the first scene, Iago and Roderigo talk about going to see Brabantio, and the second scene begins there. In the second scene, Othello and Brabantio discuss going to see the duke, and the third scene begins in the duke's chamber.

The opening dialogue between the duke and his senators indicates their high opinion of Othello, who is referred to as "valiant." Othello's first self-defense follows on the heels of Brabantio's claims of "spells and medicines." Through Othello's eloquence in this speech and in the next one, Shakespeare establishes him as a general who is also in command of his words.

In his first speech, Othello insists that he is merely a military man who lacks "the soft phrase of peace," a man who can only speak of "broil and battle." Othello uses his self-effacing words to undercut Brabantio's claims of black magic against his daughter, claims that now seem to be wild and ridiculous.

Othello's long second speech offers a touching narrative of love as he describes his own difficult and often dangerous life and Desdemona's growing fascination with it. He has had "hairbreadth" escapes, encounters with "cannibals" and was even "sold to slavery" by an "insolent foe." Is he also fascinating his audience? He definitely wins over the duke, whose opinion is further swayed by Desdemona's profession of love for and "duty" to Othello.

Shakespeare depicts Desdemona as a strong young woman in her first scene. In front of the duke, she defies her father's wishes and insists that her loyalty belongs to her new husband, Othello. In this sense Shakespeare makes her subsequent request to accompany Othello to Cyprus—during a war, no less—believable.

By already permitting us to see Iago's true colors, Shakespeare sets up the irony of Othello leaving Desdemona in his devious ensign's care. Othello's repeated use of the word "honest" to describe Iago must surely make the audience uneasy.

In the final quarter of the scene, Iago persuades Roderigo not to drown himself—not because he wants to save Roderigo, but because he wants to use Roderigo in his plan. If the audience still has any doubts about Iago's motivation, Shakespeare clears them up in this statement to Roderigo: "I have told thee often, and I retell thee again and again, I hate the Moor." In his closing soliloquy, Iago openly hatches his plot to destroy Othello.

## Act II, Scene 1

### Overview

At a seaport in Cyprus, Montano (the governor of the island) and two Cypriot gentlemen discuss the severe storm that is raging offshore. A third gentleman reveals that the Turkish fleet has been destroyed in the storm and that Cassio has arrived. All of them are worried about Othello's safety. Cassio enters and describes Othello's marriage to Desdemona, whom he praises highly. Desdemona then arrives, along with her escort Iago; his wife, Emilia; and a disguised Roderigo.

While they all wait for Othello, Iago offers some wry observation on both his own wife and women in general, and this sarcasm about women may seem more sexist than humorous to modern ears. Othello finally enters, joyously greets his wife, and announces the end of the Turkish threat to Cyprus.

After the others depart, Iago sets his plot into motion by persuading the disguised Roderigo that Desdemona is really in love with Cassio. Alone, Iago decides that his own wife, Emilia, has been the object of both Cassio's and Othello's desire. He concludes that both he and Cassio must lust after Desdemona, thereby crafting an imaginary conflict to justify his actions.

## Analysis

As this scene opens, Shakespeare enlivens his stage with the noises of the storm, cannon firings, and announcements of sail sightings. Characters once again create anticipation by referring to Othello as "brave" before he enters the scene. To increase focus on the central characters and the impending personal conflict, Shakespeare quickly resolves the military conflict over Cyprus.

Perhaps Cassio's little paean to "the divine Desdemona" seems a bit over the top. Having already established Iago's intentions, the Bard has us on the lookout for any word or event that might play into Iago's hands.

Iago is quick to focus on Cassio's affection for Desdemona, especially when Cassio takes her warmly by the hand. Iago observes, "With as little a web as this will I ensnare as great a fly as Cassio." And we know he means it!

This portrait of the actress known as La Malibran shows her in the role of Desdemona and highlights Desdemona's sweetness and femininity.

Othello's arrival and gracious greeting of his wife is a moment filled with joy and culminating in a kiss. Shakespeare will not stage a kiss again between the two characters until the end of the play—and under much different circumstances.

Left alone again with Roderigo, Iago unleashes his contorted reasoning to goad Roderigo into action. Iago's earlier barbs about women now blossom into a full assault on Desdemona's faithfulness. Even the easily persuaded Roderigo cannot believe Iago's claims at first. Through his rhetoric, Iago convinces Roderigo that Desdemona's affections for Othello will eventually fade and be redirected toward "handsome, young" Cassio.

Can we help but be impressed by the careful genius of Iago's plotting? He directs Roderigo to provoke an argument with Cassio so that Iago can incite the lieutenant's dismissal for fighting. He also convinces Roderigo that removing Cassio will benefit him on his path toward obtaining Desdemona. In his closing soliloquy, Iago announces his intention to "put the Moor / At least into a jealousy so strong / That judgment cannot cure." He claims his ultimate goal is to drive Othello "to madness."

## Act II, Scene 2

### Overview

In this mini-scene, Othello's herald enters with a proclamation: The hours between five o'clock and eleven o'clock will be devoted to feasting and revelry to celebrate the destruction of the Turkish fleet and Othello and Desdemona's "nuptial." He closes with a blessing for Cyprus and for "our noble general" Othello.

### Analysis

The word "nuptial" in this context indicates the consummation of Othello's marriage. Such a joyous proclamation would mark the end of conflict in a comedy, but *Othello* is moving in another direction.

## Act II, Scene 3

### Overview

At the castle in Cyprus, Othello asks Cassio to supervise the setting of the guard and then retires to his marriage chamber. Iago enters and persuades Cassio—who has revealed that he cannot drink—to have some wine with the other gentlemen. As Iago leads the group in some drinking songs, Cassio becomes increasingly drunk and foul-tempered. After Cassio exits, Iago tells Montano that Cassio is drunk every night.

Roderigo enters, and Iago directs him to follow Cassio. Shortly thereafter, Roderigo races back in with an angry Cassio on his heels. When Montano tries to intervene, Cassio becomes violent and wounds him with a sword.

Othello and some of his men, with weapons drawn, arrive and discover that Montano is bleeding. Appalled at what has happened, Othello strips Cassio of his title of lieutenant, saying: "Cassio I love thee; / But never more be officer of mine."

Left alone with Iago, Cassio regrets his drunken behavior and the loss of his reputation. Iago then persuades Cassio that there are "ways to recover" Othello's affection. He suggests that Cassio appeal to Desdemona to plead his case to Othello in order to restore his position. After Cassio leaves, Iago—in another soliloquy—praises the "honesty" and rationality of his advice to Cassio: Desdemona will, indeed, gladly speak for Cassio.

Left alone, Iago decides to bring his wife, Emilia, into the plot.

## Analysis

Iago behaves like a puppeteer throughout this scene, yet he is careful enough to manipulate others to act in a manner that is appropriate to their personalities. He never directly involves himself in the action.

This still from the 1995 film adaptation of *Othello* shows Iago convincing Cassio to drink in order to incite disorder within Othello's ranks.

Iago knows that Cassio, once he drinks, will be "full of quarrel and offence." He also uses Roderigo ("my sick fool") to enact his plan of exposing Cassio's darker sides to Othello. Shakespeare leaves us no choice but to be impressed by this "villain," as Iago ironically refers to himself twice in his soliloquy. Once he sets into motion the fight between Cassio and Montano, Iago can simply sit back and act as surprised as everyone else.

Iago offers further proof of his diabolical nature when he then takes Cassio into his confidence, slowly convincing the dejected soldier to pursue Desdemona's help. It would be sensible advice if only it came from another source.

In his soliloquy, Iago once again reveals the wonderfully warped reasoning that drives his actions. Iago describes his ultimate purpose for prompting Cassio to ask Desdemona to appeal to Othello: he'll "pour this pestilence" into Othello's ear to convince him that the real reason Desdemona supports Cassio is that the lieutenant is her lover.

# Act III, Scene 1

## Overview

Outside the general's quarters, Cassio directs some musicians to play a morning love song for Othello and Desdemona. A clown, sent by Othello, interrupts the music with witty remarks and an offering of money (from Othello, who wants them to stop). Cassio bribes the clown to get him an audience with Emilia, but Iago offers to take care of it. Cassio is touched and comments: "I never knew / A Florentine more kind and honest." Emilia then arrives, and Cassio asks her if she can help him to see Desdemona. She happily agrees.

## Analysis

Shakespeare uses both the music and the clown as a diversion as the plot races toward disaster. More interesting is Emilia's arrival and subsequent involvement in Cassio's predicament. Through her, we learn that Desdemona is already pleading his case before Othello.

# Act III, Scene 2

## Overview and Analysis

In this brief scene, Othello asks Iago to dispatch certain letters to Venice and then meet him at the fortifications. This seven-line scene serves merely to reinforce Othello's dependence on Iago.

In Act III, Scene 1, the clown signifies the diversions Iago uses to cover up the trouble he's causing.

# Act III, Scene 3

## Overview

On the castle grounds, Desdemona assures Cassio that she will do everything she can on his behalf with Othello. As Othello and Iago arrive, an embarrassed Cassio hurries off to avoid speaking to Othello. Iago tells Othello that the departing Cassio looked "guilty-like" as he left. Desdemona presses Othello to reconsider stripping Cassio of his title, but Othello seems preoccupied.

After Desdemona and Emilia leave, Iago tells Othello that Cassio's behavior seemed suspicious. Playing the kind counselor, Iago reminds Othello to be watchful against jealousy ("the green-eyed monster," one of Shakespeare's most famous descriptions). He also reminds Othello that Desdemona "did deceive her father" when she married him. After planting these seeds of discord, Iago leaves Othello alone. Praising Iago's "exceeding honesty," Othello laments the occurrence of adultery, which he calls the "curse of marriage" committed against "great" men.

When Desdemona and Emilia return, Othello seems distracted and complains of a headache. Desdemona offers to bind his head with a handkerchief, but he pushes it away, and it drops unnoticed to the ground as they leave. Recognizing it as an important "token" of Othello and Desdemona's early love, Emilia picks up the handkerchief. Iago, who has been asking her to steal it, snatches it from her.

When Othello reenters, he is tormented by jealousy and obsessed with thoughts of Desdemona and Cassio. Threatening Iago with death, Othello angrily insists that Iago offer proof of Desdemona's infidelity. In addition

Iago takes Desdemona's lost handkerchief from his wife, Emilia, thus setting into motion the final, dark stages of his plan.

to suggesting Cassio was having lewd dreams about Desdemona, Iago says that he saw Cassio wipe his beard with the very handkerchief that was Othello's "first gift" to Desdemona.

In the scene's final moments Othello and Iago kneel as Othello asks Iago (whom he now calls "lieutenant") to murder Cassio within three days. Othello then vows to find some "swift means of death" for "the fair devil," Desdemona.

## Analysis

The play's entire tragedy turns on this pivotal scene, and Shakespeare crafts one of his finest scenes of verbal seduction as Iago convinces Othello that his wife has been unfaithful. Though Desdemona's support of Cassio could not be more genuine, Iago returns to Brabantio's warning: "She did deceive her father."

Racial elements also surface in Iago's rhetoric. He even associates the "unnatural" with loving people of another "complexion"—to Othello's face, no less! Othello seems slowly to crack before our eyes. He begins to question everything about himself, including his age and social standing. The marriage he once cherished now becomes a "curse."

Despite Emilia's retrieval of the handkerchief and her giving it to Iago, Shakespeare does not implicate her in Iago's destructive intentions. Once she leaves, Iago begins plotting to plant the handkerchief in Cassio's lodging.

By the time Othello returns to the stage, he is wracked with doubt and suspicion: "I think my wife be honest, and think she is not." Iago claims he is motivated by "foolish honesty and love" to tell Othello everything. His reenactment of Cassio's supposed sexual dream about Desdemona provides one of the play's most disturbing moments. The mention of the handkerchief as Iago's ultimate "proof" of Desdemona's infidelity fills Othello with feelings of vengeance.

In the final act of kneeling between Iago and Othello, Shakespeare unites the two characters in a twisted scene of devotion. As they pledge their allegiance to each other, Iago agrees to murder Cassio, and Othello announces that he will find some "swift means of death" for Desdemona. Iago has finally gotten what he wanted. Othello tells him: "Now art thou my lieutenant." Something sinister attends Iago's final pledge to Othello: "I am your own for ever."

## Act III, Scene 4

### Overview

At the castle, Desdemona asks the clown where Cassio is, and the two exchange witticisms. Desdemona then realizes that she has lost the treasured handkerchief

In a scene of ominous irony, Iago pledges his allegiance to Othello just as Othello pledges to kill his wife, Desdemona.

Othello gave to her. She tells Emilia she is not worried, however, because Othello is "made of no such baseness / As jealous creatures are."

Othello arrives and demands to see the handkerchief. When Desdemona says she does not have it with her, he describes it as a magic heirloom given to his mother by an Egyptian "charmer." Desdemona tries to hide its loss by changing the subject to Cassio, which sends Othello into a rage, and he leaves. Iago then enters with Cassio, who asks if Desdemona has convinced Othello to return Cassio to his lieutenancy. Desdemona explains that she must postpone her efforts because Othello seems "altered." Iago acts surprised at the news of Othello's anger and leaves to speak to him. Emilia reiterates previous thoughts about jealousy: "'Tis a monster / Begot upon itself, born on itself."

While Cassio waits for more news, the courtesan Bianca arrives and asks why she has not heard from him.

He assures her that everything will return to normal when he is no longer burdened by "leaden thoughts." Cassio then shows Bianca the handkerchief he found in his room; he requests that she copy its design and she agrees. Cassio asks her to leave, as he does not want Othello to see him "womaned."

## Analysis

Just as Othello unravels in the previous scene, Desdemona's sense of security begins to fade as this scene progresses. Desdemona's insistence that Othello is free from all jealous feelings sets up Othello's entrance. He is a study in distrust and suspicion as he demands to see the handkerchief.

Othello behaves more like Iago in this scene: he is manipulative and deceitful, and he even makes sexually loaded comments about the "liberal" nature of Desdemona's heart. His speech about the handkerchief's origins seems fabricated solely to make her feel guilty. His words in this scene are also prophetic; the handkerchief's loss does lead to disaster.

Even though she knows about the handkerchief, Emilia stands silently by watching this horror unfold. "I know not, madam," she tells Desdemona, when asked how the handkerchief could have been lost. Is she simply shocked? Because we have no indication that Emilia is involved in her husband's machinations, Shakespeare leaves her behavior open to interpretation.

Shakespeare has us on alert when Cassio asks Bianca to make a copy of the embroidered handkerchief's pattern. What unintended devilry will come from this request?

# Act IV, Scene 1

## Overview

Iago taunts Othello with crass images of Desdemona "naked ... in bed" with Cassio. He further torments Othello by bringing up the handkerchief and implying that Cassio has boasted of sleeping with Desdemona. Othello finally faints from distress. Cassio enters, but Iago tells him to return after Othello's fit of "epilepsy" has passed. Iago then places Othello within earshot of a conversation between Iago and Cassio. Knowing that Othello will believe they are talking about Desdemona, Iago goads Cassio on to speak about his amorous escapades with Bianca.

Bianca arrives, complaining about having to copy the embroidered handkerchief, which she angrily returns to Cassio. After they leave, Iago tells Othello that Cassio has been joking publicly about his affair with Desdemona and has given her handkerchief to a common whore. Othello is enraged, but his words also indicate that he still has some affection for Desdemona.

Iago says he will be Cassio's "undertaker" and suggests that Othello strangle Desdemona in the very bed she has "contaminated." Othello responds, "The justice of it pleases."

Lodovico, one of Desdemona's relatives, arrives from Venice with orders from the Venetian Senate that Othello should return to Venice and leave Cassio in his place in Cyprus. Desdemona, who has entered with Lodovico, begins to speak in Cassio's favor. While Othello reads the letter, he calls her "devil" repeatedly and, in a rage, he strikes her in front of the others. Lodovico is dumbfounded and asks Iago whether Othello has gone mad or whether the message from Venice has upset him. Iago replies that Othello is "much changed."

### Analysis

Whereas Roderigo seemed to play the dupe in earlier scenes, Othello now appears to be putty in Iago's hands. He is open to every one of Iago's suggestions and believes every foul lie about both Desdemona and Cassio. His obsessive focus on the handkerchief feeds his association of Desdemona's supposed infidelity with the lost object. At one point in his frenzy he exclaims, "Handkerchief–confessions–handkerchief!"

Through Othello's increasing horror at hearing Iago's lies about Desdemona and Cassio, Shakespeare builds to the explosion, which results in Othello striking his innocent wife. Lodovico's final words indicate that he feels "deceived" by Othello's former goodness; he no longer believes in "the noble Moor."

## Act IV, Scene 2

### Overview

In a conversation with Othello inside the castle, Emilia defends Desdemona's character as "honest, chaste, and true." She insists that some "wretch" must have put these thoughts of Desdemona's dishonesty into Othello's head. Othello directs her to bring Desdemona to him, but once she leaves, he rejects Emilia's heartfelt defense of his wife. He then directs Emilia to wait outside the door, like a "bawd" in a brothel, as he interrogates Desdemona.

As Othello accuses Desdemona of being a "false" wife, she tries in vain to defend her honor. Questioning her in a cruel manner, he accuses her of being a "whore" and a "strumpet." Although Othello weeps at the thought of what his wife has supposedly done and the loss of their love, he refuses to believe her when she protests that she is innocent. Finally, he calls Emilia back into the room, pays her for standing guard, and leaves.

Overcome with grief, Desdemona asks Emilia to fetch Iago and then asks him for help with her predicament. As Emilia describes Othello's odious behavior to Iago, she begins to rail against the "eternal villain" and "insinuating rogue" who must have put false thoughts of infidelity in Othello's mind. Emilia insists that some "villainous knave" has "abused" Othello and should be whipped for what he has done. Iago abruptly tells Emilia to shut up and tries to convince Desdemona that the stress of his office is simply wearing on Othello.

As the two women exit, Roderigo enters. He is angry with Iago for avoiding him. Claiming he has been made a fool of, he accuses Iago of doing nothing to aid in his effort to win back Desdemona—despite all the jewels he has given Iago to give to Desdemona. Roderigo threatens to ask for his gifts back, but Iago insists that some hope remains for Roderigo's suit. He informs Roderigo that Cassio is to replace Othello in command at Cyprus and that Othello and Desdemona will soon leave for Mauritania. Iago then convinces Roderigo that they can stop her departure only by "removing" Cassio, by "knocking out his brains," so that Othello will have to stay in Cyprus. They devise a plan to attack Cassio around midnight while he is dining with Bianca.

Othello is convinced that Desdemona is cheating on him, but even as he accuses her, he holds out hope that she's been faithful.

## Analysis

Othello's treatment of both women as prostitutes in a brothel is tasteless and insulting. Yet, even while he accuses Desdemona of being a whore, he also reveals some flicker of the love he still has left for her, especially in his weeping over what he believes has happened. At one point when Desdemona insists she is not a "whore," Othello shows a brief sign of wavering. "Is't possible?" he asks. Shakespeare wisely leaves some glimmer of Othello's goodness. Otherwise, the character would become completely repulsive, and there would be no tragedy.

The play's dramatic irony thickens as a desperate Desdemona turns to Iago for help. At this point in the action, Iago's assurances that "all things shall be well" have an insidious ring to them. Emilia's increasing anger at the "villain" responsible for poisoning Othello's mind infuriates Iago. Still he reveals no second thoughts, no qualms, about what he has done. Iago is Shakespeare's one villain who is completely devoid of any remorse.

Iago manages to turn Roderigo's righteous anger against the poor fool. We know that Iago has kept Roderigo's jewels for himself. Shakespeare conveys a comic undertone in the fool's indignation, but this humor is undercut by Iago's closing plot to enlist Roderigo's aid in killing Cassio.

## Act IV, Scene 3

### Overview

While walking with Lodovico and some attendants, Othello orders Desdemona to prepare for bed and to dismiss Emilia as well. Left alone, the two women prepare Desdemona's bed. Emilia says she has followed Desdemona's orders and dressed the bed with sheets from her wedding night. Desdemona directs Emilia to wrap her in one of the sheets as a shroud if she should die before Emilia.

The two women discuss marital infidelity and whether they would ever be unfaithful to their husbands. Desdemona cannot believe any woman would commit adultery, regardless of the price, but Emilia insists that women are as capable as men of misdeeds in their marriage.

### Analysis

In a previous scene, Iago had directed Othello to murder Desdemona in her bed. Othello's directing her at the

This still from Orson Welles's 1952 adaptation of *Othello* shows Desdemona in such distress that she appeals to the villainous Iago.

beginning of this scene to go to bed and to dismiss Emilia creates an immediate sense of discomfort. Despite her discussions of death and sadness, Desdemona remains firm in her love for Othello.

The conversation about unfaithfulness in marriage between Desdemona and Emilia reflects both their age and their character. Youthful and pure in spirit, Desdemona still believes that all women are faithful to their husbands. World-weary and coming from another social class, the more experienced Emilia contends that women are just as capable of infidelity as men. In fact, she thinks it would be better if men knew that their wives "have sense like them"—that women have the same affections, desires, and weaknesses as men. Emilia concludes that women learn their own misbehavior from the "ills" of their men.

## Act V, Scene 1

### Overview

Iago and Roderigo meet on a street in Cyprus where, hiding behind a shop front, they are waiting to attack Cassio. As Cassio walks by, Roderigo attacks him but fails to hurt him because Cassio is wearing a shirt of mail (a metal chain-link fabric). Cassio then stabs and wounds Roderigo in the leg. Iago jumps out from his hiding place and wounds Cassio in the leg.

Othello—who enters just in time to hear Cassio's cries of "Murder! Murder!"—believes that Iago has kept his promise to kill Cassio. Othello then runs off to kill Desdemona in her "lust-stained" bed.

Lodovico and Gratiano, another one of Desdemona's Venetian relatives, hear Cassio and Roderigo crying out for help but are hesitant to get involved. Iago returns to

Théodore Chassériau's depiction of Desdemona shows the bond between the young newlywed and her handmaid.

the scene with a lantern and pretends that he has suddenly heard the wounded men's cries. Iago stabs Roderigo and kills him, then enlists Lodovico and Gratiano's help with Cassio.

Bianca arrives, but when she bemoans what has happened to Cassio, Iago accuses her of having been part of the plot to hurt Cassio. Iago tells the others: "I do suspect this trash / To be a party in this injury." While Iago continues to point the finger of blame at innocent Bianca, the wounded Cassio is carried off in a chair. When Emilia enters and discovers that Cassio has been hurt, she joins Iago in insulting Bianca as a "strumpet."

## Analysis

Iago reveals the full extent of his expedience with others' lives when he remarks that it really does not matter whether Cassio or Roderigo dies. "Every way makes my gain," he observes. Iago admits to having swindled the jewels from Roderigo, and he has no intention of returning them.

Despite Iago's ingenious plotting and his control over many of the characters, he also displays a few signs of worry in this scene. When Cassio's hidden shirt of mail saves him from being killed, Iago contemplates what will happen if Cassio survives. He fears that Cassio's natural reputation ("a daily beauty in his life") may make Iago look "ugly." Iago realizes that, now more than ever, Cassio "must die"—or Othello might reveal Iago's plans to Cassio and thereby expose Iago.

Alone on stage Iago notes: "This is the night / That either makes me or fordoes me quite."

Iago's evil runs so deep he doesn't care which of his "friends" dies—remarking that "every way makes [his] gain."

# Act V, Scene 2

## Overview

Othello enters the bedchamber where Desdemona sleeps and speaks of the "cause" of "justice" he is about to enact. As he kisses his wife and she awakens, Othello bids her to say her final prayers.

Realizing that he plans to murder her, Desdemona insists on her innocence and pleads for her life. She tries to defend Cassio and to tell the truth about the handkerchief, but Othello–thinking that "honest Iago" has killed Cassio–refuses to believe her. Finally, he smothers her, though she is not actually dead yet.

Emilia calls at the door. Once Othello lets her enter, she tells him that Cassio is not dead. Hearing her mistress's moans, Emilia then discovers Desdemona in the throes of death. Desdemona, remaining faithful to Othello, refuses to name him as her murderer. Then she dies.

At first Othello denies having killed Desdemona, but then he admits what he has done. Once Othello reveals that it was Iago who informed him of Desdemona's infidelity, Emilia realizes what her husband has done. Emilia cries "Murder," bringing Iago, Montano, and Gratiano racing into the room.

When Emilia explains the truth about the handkerchief, Othello tries to kill Iago but only wounds him. As Iago flees, he fatally stabs Emilia. Lodovico, Montano, and some officers return with Iago as their prisoner and Cassio (still recuperating in a chair). Letters found on Roderigo's body reveal Iago's involvement in the plot and clear Cassio of any wrongdoing.

Now aware that he was mistaken all along about Desdemona, Othello stabs himself and falls on the bed next to her. As the play ends, Lodovico directs Cassio to "torture" the "hellish villain" Iago.

## Analysis

In his final murderous moments, Othello still exhibits some love for Desdemona. Although he is compelled to kiss her, his overstimulated sense of doling out justice for his wife's infidelity drives his actions. Even in death, Desdemona remains strong, insisting on her innocence, trying to reason with her enraged husband, and refusing to blame him for murdering her. She is one of Shakespeare's purest creations. Emilia calls her "the sweetest innocent."

Iago's treacherous influence on Othello seems apparent when Othello at first lies to Emilia about Desdemona's

Only after Othello has murdered his wife, Desdemona, does he realize her innocence and Iago's evil.

death. Emilia's loyalty to Desdemona shines in this scene, as does her indignation over what Iago has done. The name "villain" is finally and properly assigned to Iago, and Lodovico also refers to him as "this slave."

It's an undeniably busy scene, with stabbings that are both wounding and fatal, quick entrances and exits, and almost all the major characters on stage. Othello's final description of himself as "one that loved not wisely, but too well" has become one of the play's most quoted lines. In what seems like a desperate attempt to reinstate his reputation, Othello's final words describe one of his military conquests. Cassio, offering one small tribute to the dying Othello, says that the general was "great of heart."

## List of Major Characters

- Othello, the Moor of Venice and protagonist of the play
- Iago, Othello's ensign, sometimes referred to as his "ancient"
- Desdemona, a Venetian lady and Othello's wife
- Emilia, Iago's wife and attendant to Desdemona
- Cassio, Othello's lieutenant
- Roderigo, a Venetian gentleman
- Brabantio, Desdemona's father and a member of the Venetian Senate
- Duke of Venice
- Bianca, a courtesan, in love with Cassio
- Montano, the governor of Cyprus
- Gratiano, a Venetian nobleman and Brabantio's brother
- Lodovico, a Venetian nobleman and relative to Brabantio
- The clown, a comic servant to Othello and Desdemona
- Herald, officers, servants, attendants, messengers, musicians, torchbearers

## Analysis of Major Characters

### Othello

Shakespeare crafted one of his most complex tragic heroes in Othello. The brave, self-assured general we meet at the beginning of the play seems to bear little resemblance to the tortured, ruined man who has lost everything dear to him at the end. As the play progresses, we watch the accomplished general slowly unravel before our eyes.

Othello is a respected military leader held in high esteem by the Venetian Senate. In both character and reputation, Othello seems like a decisive man who is bound for further greatness. Othello's command of the scene when Brabantio brings charges against him shows that he has a level head in a potentially dangerous situation. How can we not admire this man of action who has survived slavery and so many near-death dangers?

On the other hand, Othello possesses a certain naïve and trusting attitude toward others. Othello's repeated use of the word "honest" to describe Iago seems to betray a certain lack of perception. Is it also a clue to Othello's sudden mistrust of his young, faithful wife that he has so obviously misjudged Iago? Othello is so sure of Iago's loyalty, and so sure in the beginning of Desdemona's love, that little room exists in his mind for life's grayer and less obvious areas.

One of the sources of Othello's complexity is his place as an outsider in Venetian society. As an African Moor, Othello–although he is respected for his military deeds–is mistrusted for his ethnicity. Throughout the play, Iago, Roderigo, and Brabantio openly insult Othello's race. Brabantio feels no qualms about accusing Othello of witchcraft in front of the Senate.

The play's dual setting also reflects on Othello's character and behavior. Othello has been in Venice, a city of high culture, for only a few months. As he observes early in the play, he is more accustomed to the "tented field" of military battles. Is the more impulsive Othello

Although the play takes on the unfairness Othello faces because of his race, historically only white actors were allowed to perform the role.

we encounter in the colony of Cyprus closer to his true personality?

Once Othello allows Iago's accusations to influence him, his personality becomes obsessive. The love he has so strongly proclaimed for Desdemona unravels almost immediately in his mind, and he begins to accept and to look for every possibility of his wife's infidelity. Othello's jealousy is so strong that it moves him to madness. Othello places so much value on the handkerchief that his wife supposedly gave Cassio that he seems to transfer his affection from his wife to an object. The handkerchief, a "pledge of love" he gave to Desdemona, also carries the weight of Othello's heritage. As he points out in the final scene, it was "an antique token" that his father gave to his mother.

Despite Othello's flaws, one of the main sources for the play's overwhelming tragedy is that, even to the end, he exhibits signs of his love for his wife. His inner conflict is so strong that at one point in the play he faints. However, as the final scene reveals, Othello's love for Desdemona is no match for the overblown sense of "justice" that he repeatedly refers to as his "cause." The idealistic soldier we met earlier in the play now places ideals above people.

## Iago

The villain of *Othello*, Iago commands the stage from his first appearance. Even when he is not on stage, his haunting figure dominates the play. It is certainly no accident that Shakespeare chose to introduce the vengeful Iago before Othello. Shakespeare lends a disturbing importance to his villainous creation, making Iago one of the most famous and most desirable dramatic roles in history.

Iago may also have his origins in the "Vice character" from the morality plays of the Middle Ages. Vice characters usually tempt others into misbehaving and then take pleasure in the consequences suffered by these people who were once good. Whereas the Vice characters were often comic, closer to Shakespeare's Falstaff, Iago remains evil throughout *Othello*. Iago's speech in Act I, in which he mocks the value of "virtue," indicates his immoral character and his association with the Vice figure.

On the surface, Iago's motivation seems apparent. He has lost the lieutenancy to Cassio and resents being

Because of his dogged commitment to ruining Othello, Iago is known as one of the greatest villains of all time.

reduced to Othello's "ancient" (or ensign). Iago's early comments indicate that he believes he has been swindled out of the position he deserves and is now trapped in a lower social position.

Iago also quickly establishes the deceptive nature of his personality. Insisting that his actions will never reveal his intentions, he tells Roderigo, "I am not what I am." Iago openly insults his master, Othello: "I do hate him as I do hell-pains." In his first encounter with Othello, however, he is pledging his love and loyalty to the general.

Iago is a master of manipulation, goading the foolish Roderigo, a gentleman of higher social position, into causing a ruckus to rouse Desdemona's father. Throughout the play Iago cleverly uses Roderigo for his own purposes. Iago works his way into Othello's confidence and then slowly and carefully persuades him that Desdemona has been unfaithful with Cassio. He has no qualms about killing others to get what he wants.

In his initial scene with Desdemona and Emilia, he further shows his base values when he paints a deceitful portrait of women in general. While his words seem to be in jest, they also serve as a disturbing warning of his disregard for women, which is proven when Iago goads Othello on in killing Desdemona. Perhaps even more astonishing is when he uses Emilia in his plot to destroy Othello and in the final scene kills his own wife when she reveals the crimes he has committed.

Watching Iago's villainy working on Othello's peace of mind is one of *Othello*'s most enjoyable aspects, because we know the character is a wicked mastermind. In every scene—with every sinister word—Iago holds our undivided attention.

Iago is also a master of rhetoric who knows the sheer power of words and readily employs them to his own advantage, such as convincing Roderigo that he has a chance with Desdemona or persuading Othello that Desdemona is untrue. Iago constructs his own reasons for his actions, reasons that often have no basis in reality, for example, claiming that Othello has slept with his wife. As he openly admits, Iago uses these fabrications to feed his "revenge."

## Desdemona

The young bride of Othello, Desdemona, is central to the main conflict of the play.

In all of her scenes Desdemona acts out of the kindness of her heart with every character that surrounds her. She is both the object of her husband's love and the victim of his jealousy. More importantly, she is a character who never wavers in her love for her husband or in defense of her reputation. Desdemona may seem weak or secondary, but her goodness becomes strength in a tragedy that focuses on the power struggle between good and evil.

Like Juliet in *Romeo and Juliet* and Jessica in *The Merchant of Venice*, Desdemona defies her father to pursue her romantic interest. Her father, Brabantio, reflecting the prejudiced views of Venetian society, says that her love for Othello is "against all rules of nature," but his objections do not stop her.

Modern audiences may also notice another streak of defiance in Desdemona, who openly announces that she "did love the Moor to live with him." Desdemona is surprisingly open about her sensuality. There is nothing shy or retiring about this young woman. She even asks the duke if she may accompany Othello on his military mission to Cyprus. The world Desdemona encounters in Cyprus is very different from the wealthy, cultured one she leaves behind in Venice.

At one point in the play, Cassio refers to Desdemona as "our great captain's captain." Desdemona also quickly exchanges witty remarks with Iago in her first encounter with him. She seems capable of holding her own with anyone. Her support for Cassio indicates her strong sense of loyalty. She readily takes up his case and speaks on his behalf: out of the goodness of her heart, she pleads with Othello to reinstate Cassio after he is dismissed for fighting.

On the other hand, Desdemona also displays signs of her youth and naïveté. In her conversation with Emilia about women and infidelity, Desdemona cannot accept the idea that women can be unfaithful to their husbands. "I do not think there is any such woman," she says to

Even when faced with Othello's murderous rage, Desdemona is unflinching in her commitment to her husband.

Emilia. Desdemona also tells Emilia that she believes Othello does not possess a jealous nature: "I think the sun where he was born / Drew all such humors from him." Yet, the Othello we encounter as the play progresses is mad with jealousy. How well does Desdemona really know her husband?

Desdemona's love for her husband is her strongest motivation. She proclaims her love for Othello to the very end–even in the last scene in which he kills her. Her final words do not point the finger at Othello; instead she claims that her killer was "Nobody–I myself." Is this foolishness or fidelity? Over the centuries. actors have played Desdemona in a number of ways, from innocent and girlish to strong and feisty.

The "divine" Desdemona, as Cassio refers to her, continues to fascinate and challenge the actors who play her.

## Emilia

Emilia, Iago's wife, provides the voice of reason in *Othello*—although her wisest comments come late in the play. She also offers the strongest defense of Desdemona's character, but her words to Othello fall on deaf ears. Throughout many of her scenes Emilia reveals wisdom and understanding that Shakespeare grants to no other character in this tragedy.

Emilia's loyalties are somewhat divided between Iago and Desdemona. Until she realizes what her husband has done, Emilia remains loyal to Iago throughout much of the tragedy. She endures his snide remarks about wives and women in general and is clever enough to offer her own responses. When she finds Desdemona's lost handkerchief, she gives it to Iago (who has frequently asked for it). Yet she also worries that its loss will upset Desdemona and tries to compel Iago to return it to her.

Emilia's comments on jealousy in Act III, Scene 4 accurately describe the terrible change in Othello's character. She observes how jealousy feeds on itself and becomes its own cause. "'Tis a monster / Begot upon itself, born on itself," she tells Desdemona. Shakespeare appears to be using Emilia to reflect one of the play's basic themes. When Othello confronts Emilia about his wife's infidelity, she says that she would "lay down" her soul that Desdemona is "honest, chaste, and true."

Emilia's more worldly character also serves as a contrast to Desdemona's innocence. Emilia's speech about women being just as capable of disloyalty as men seems quite modern and enlightened for Shakespeare's time. She says, "Let husbands know / Their wives have sense like them." Desdemona cannot accept the thought that

Contrasting Desdemona's naïve innocence, Emilia proves to be a skeptic when it comes to love and relationships.

women can also be unfaithful, but the more experienced Emilia insists that women have the same "affections" and "desires" as men.

In the tragedy's final scene, Shakespeare uses Emilia's voice to reveal the sad truth to Othello. Realizing that Othello has killed her "sweet mistress," overcoming her duty to her husband, Emilia insists that Iago has lied to Othello about Desdemona's unfaithfulness. Emilia also displays no sign of weakness or fear toward Othello or any other man in the play. "I care not for thy sword," she tells him once she exposes what he has done.

Shakespeare also uses Emilia to confront Iago and to expose him at the end. She refuses to listen to her husband when he tells her not to speak. After she says she will not let "heaven and men and devils" stop her from telling the truth about his villainous lies, Iago kills her for being honest. In more modern productions, Emilia's character has received more force and attention.

Chapter Three

# A Closer Look

It's easy to get sucked into Shakespeare's dramatic plots and emotional characters, thus missing the rich layers of historical references, moral or ideological lessons, and recurring symbols. Some of these important elements in Shakespeare's plays can even get lost in the language. Shakespeare's lasting contribution to English is his unique and remarkable phrasing, but it has proven to be one of the greatest challenges to audiences (both today and in Shakespeare's time). Shakespeare's vocabulary was huge, full of references to the Bible as well as Greek and Roman mythology. Yet his most brilliant phrases often combine very simple and familiar words: "to be or not to be," for example. Four centuries after Shakespeare lived, to speak English is to quote him. His huge vocabulary and linguistic fertility are still astonishing. We may wonder how it is even possible for a single human being to say so many memorable things. This chapter examines

James Earl Jones played Othello in 1981.

Shakespeare's use of language in *Othello*, the themes of the play, and its deeper meanings.

## Shakespeare's Words

Shakespeare has shaped modern English far more than any other writer. So why do so many English-speaking readers find his language so difficult? It is our language, too, but it has changed so much that it is no longer familiar. Just imagine, he would probably have some difficulty understanding us, too! Many of our everyday words and phrases would baffle him, even common expressions such as *what's up,* or *that's cool.*

If it would be so hard to communicate with him, how can we call him "the greatest master of the English language"? Many of the words of Shakespeare's time have become archaic. Words like "thou," "thee," "thy," "thyself," and "thine," which were among the most common words in the language in Shakespeare's day, have all but disappeared today.

Sometimes the same words now have different meanings. We are apt to be misled by such simple, familiar words as "kind," "wonderful," "waste," "just," and "dear," which he often uses in ways that differ from our usage.

Often a glossary and footnotes will solve these problems for us. But it is most important to bear in mind that even in his own time, Shakespeare's rich language was challenging. And this was deliberate. Shakespeare was inventing his own kind of English. It remains unique today.

A child doesn't learn to talk by using a dictionary. Children learn first by sheer immersion. Dictionaries can help us later, when we already speak and read the language well (and learn more slowly).

The best way to learn Shakespeare is not to depend on the footnotes and glossary too much, but instead to be like a baby: just get into the flow of the language. Go to performances of the plays or watch movies of them. The language has a magical way of teaching itself, if we let it. There is no reason to feel stupid or frustrated when it doesn't come easily.

Only the King James translation of the Bible, perhaps, has had a more profound and pervasive influence on the English language than Shakespeare. And, of course, the Bible was written by many authors over many centuries, and the King James translation, published in 1611, was the combined effort of many scholars.

## Characters' Language

Often when we meet someone for the first time we learn a lot about them just from the way they talk. It's no different with a character in a book, movie, or play. Just as Shakespeare's rich language can cause excitement and confusion in equal measure, the way his characters speak expresses volumes about who they are and where they come from. Othello's use of language differs from that of the villain Iago, for example, and it's no accident.

### Iago's Golden Tongue

Although Othello has some powerful speeches, including his inspiring descriptions of his youthful military life and his early declarations of love for Desdemona, Shakespeare reserves the play's most impressive language for Iago. Because Iago is a master of rhetoric, he is particularly adroit at using words for his own purposes. Note that Shakespeare has Iago speak in prose when he is manipulating Roderigo and verse when conniving with Othello.

Many of the most quoted lines from *Othello* belong to Iago; some of his observations have become proverbial in their usage. Centuries after it was invented, his remark about "the green-eyed monster" is still a recognizable metaphor for jealousy. In a frequently quoted observation, Iago comments on the price of losing one's good reputation: "Who steals my purse steals trash ... / But he that filches from me my good name / Robs me of that which not enriches him / And makes me poor indeed." This extended metaphor also carries a great deal of irony—the most notorious thief in the play is Iago!

As rhetoric, Iago's arguments may make sense on one level—but a closer look reveals his twisted reasoning. Shakespeare fills Iago's speeches, especially his soliloquies, with bold and suggestive imagery that illustrates his warped logic. Iago's soliloquy at the end of Act II, Scene 1 offers a fine example:

> ***That Cassio loves her, I do well believe't;***
> ***That she loves him, 'tis apt and of great credit.***
> ***The Moor, howbeit that I endure him not,***
> ***Is of a constant, loving, noble nature,***
> ***And I dare think he'll prove to Desdemona***
> ***A most dear husband. Now I do love her too;***
> ***Not out of absolute lust, though peradventure***
> ***I stand accountant for as great a sin,***
> ***But partly led to diet my revenge,***
> ***For that I do suspect the lusty Moor***
> ***Hath leaped into my seat; the thought whereof***

> ***Doth, like a poisonous mineral, gnaw my inwards;***
> ***And nothing can or shall content my soul***
> ***Till I am evened with him, wife for wife ...***

Iago begins this speech by stating three simple facts: Cassio loves Desdemona, Desdemona loves him back in an acceptable and admirable fashion, and Othello has a true and loyal nature. Iago repeats his view of Othello's loyalty by commenting that the Moor will make a "most dear husband" to Desdemona. A pun on "dear" occurs in its double meaning of (1) a loving husband, and (2) an expensive one. If Iago's plotting succeeds it will, indeed, cost Desdemona her life–an expensive price to pay. Notice also Iago's use of words associated with money: "credit," "dear," "accountant." Resentful and envious, he is always keeping score and thinking in monetary terms. His repeated use of the word "purse" throughout the play reinforces his mercantile attitudes. Because Iago also needs a motivation, he invents one: midway through the speech he decides that he also loves Desdemona. Yet it is not his "lust" for Desdemona that defines his sin but his desire to use her in his vengeful plot–to feed ("diet") his revenge, as he says. Iago then claims that "lusty" Othello "hath leapt into my seat." The metaphoric use of the word "seat" holds a number of meanings here, including Iago's rightful "place" as a husband with Emilia and the saddle on a horse.

Iago fabricates a new motivation for hating Othello: the Moor has slept with Emilia. Iago employs one of many similes when he states that the thought of Othello stealing his "place" with Emilia eats away at his innards "like a poisonous mineral." Shakespeare loves to repeat his imagery, especially within each play. Iago's simile recalls Brabantio's earlier accusation that Othello had used "drugs or minerals" to seduce Desdemona. Shakespeare imparts a certain irony to the final words of his master rhetorician. Iago states: "From this time forth I never will speak word."

## A Way with Words

Shakespeare's remarkable dexterity with words alongside his many references to mythology and history have caused some to wonder if the humble Bard from Stratford-upon-Avon is the true author of "Shakespeare's" plays. Even the great American author Mark Twain thought the plays' true author was too well educated and knowledgeable to have been the modestly schooled man from Stratford. Many answers have been given, but the three leading candidates are Francis Bacon, Christopher Marlowe, and Edward de Vere.

Bacon was a distinguished lawyer, scientist, philosopher, and essayist. Many considered him one of the great geniuses of his time, capable of any literary achievement, though he wrote little poetry and, as far as we know, no dramas. When people began to suspect that "Shakespeare" was only a pen name, he seemed like a natural candidate. But his writing style was vastly different from the style of the plays. Marlowe, on the other hand, wrote several excellent tragedies in a style much like that of the Shakespeare tragedies, though without the comic blend. But he was reportedly killed in a mysterious incident in 1593, before most of the Bard's plays existed. Could his death have been faked? Is it possible that he lived on for decades in hiding, writing under a pen name? This is what his advocates contend.

Finally, Edward de Vere, Earl of Oxford, is now the most popular and plausible alternative to the lad from Stratford. He had a high reputation as a poet and playwright in his day, but his life was full of scandal. That controversial life seems to match what the poet says about himself in the sonnets, as well as many events in the plays (especially *Hamlet*). However, he died in 1604, and most scholars believe this rules him out as the author of plays that were published after that date. The great majority of experts reject these and all other alternative candidates, sticking with the traditional view, affirmed in the 1623 First Folio of the plays, that the author was the man from Stratford. That remains the safest position to take, unless startling new evidence turns up, which, at this late date, seems highly unlikely.

## Themes

The theme, or message, of a play is just as important as its plot. By understanding the deeper ideas Shakespeare is trying to convey through the events of Othello, those events take on a new, more robust significance. A work of literature may have major and minor themes running throughout, and no doubt this is the case in *Othello*. As Shakespeare develops each character's motivation, he also develops the central themes of his play.

### The Difference Between Appearance and Reality

Just as Shakespeare's phrasing slips between conflicting descriptions and strange metaphors, one of Shakespeare's main themes and central conflict in *Othello* is the difference between appearance and reality. The play explores the terrible tragedy that results when a basically good character can no longer discern the difference between what actually is and what only seems to be.

Othello is so strongly manipulated by Iago into believing that Desdemona has been unfaithful that he stops believing in his wife. Although it may appear that Desdemona has been untrue—thanks in great part to Iago's lies—Othello fails to question the evidence. Instead he accepts the appearance of infidelity as the truth. His obsession with the appearance of unfaithfulness leads Othello into madness and revenge.

In an ironic twist on the theme, Othello believes in his wicked ensign, Iago, more than he believes in his wife. Iago offers Othello the appearance of support and loyalty, yet in reality he works constantly to bring down Othello. Iago believes he can rely on Othello to trust him because—as he says—Othello has "a free and open nature / That thinks men honest that but seem to be so."

To make matters worse, Othello begins to view his wife's goodness as an act, as if she only appears to be innocent. Believing Iago's lies, Othello accuses the most "honest" person in his life—his wife—of being "false," yet he repeatedly refers to Iago as "honest."

Shakespeare emphasizes the force of this theme by allowing his audience to know the truth and to see the difference between appearance and reality. At every turn, we hear Iago's true intentions: we know that his words are lies and that his loyalty to Othello is only an act. While the characters become caught in a dangerous web, the audience always knows the truth. In this way, the Bard reinforces his major theme, along with the tragedy of what happens.

## The Destructive Nature of Jealousy

In *Othello,* jealousy serves as a destructive power that destroys real love and can leave a jealous person alone and ruined. This theme is so prominent in the play that a recently identified psychological disorder, called Othello Syndrome, is used to describe one who is obsessed with the idea that their spouse is cheating on them without having proof.

Emilia's comments on jealousy in Act III indicate the play's major premise. Jealousy is a part of human nature: when it takes over, a person loses all sense of reason. Emilia's comment that jealousy is a monster "born on itself" applies to both Iago and Othello. Iago is driven by his jealousy for Cassio, who has received the lieutenant position that Iago feels he deserved. Othello's jealousy feeds on itself throughout the play and eventually drives him to madness and murder.

In an ironic twist, it is Iago who first warns Othello about jealousy. "It is the green-eyed monster," he tells Othello while he plants the seeds of jealousy in the general's open mind. Iago knows the effect of jealousy and that "trifles light as air" can be proof enough to a jealous mind. Using this knowledge, he masterminds the play's tragic events.

Shakespeare also reinforces the notion that jealousy is mostly hidden. Othello's jealous nature seems to escape most of the characters, except, of course, for Iago, who plays on it. When Emilia asks Desdemona if Othello is jealous, Desdemona responds that it is not in his nature. Yet, almost all of his actions are predicated on his jealousy.

Does awareness of age also contribute to jealousy—especially when one person is much older than the other? The age difference between Othello and Desdemona may also play a factor in his jealousy. Othello points out in Act III that he has "declined / Into the vale of years," meaning he has become older. In his final speech, Othello insists he was not "easily jealous" and claims instead that he "loved not wisely, but too well."

## The Conflict Between Passion and Reason

One of the most universal themes appearing in *Othello* is the conflict between passion and reason. Most people can relate to the strong feelings exhibited by the main characters: love, jealousy, envy, and hate. In *Othello*, Shakespeare illustrates what happens when passion get the better of his characters' reason.

Early in the play, when Iago tries to stop Roderigo from drowning himself, he tells him that "we have reason" to control our emotions and our lust. Iago suggests that instead of killing himself, Roderigo should use his rational mind to overcome his strong desires for Desdemona. Iago's arguments also lead to his racist accusations that "Moors" are "changeable in their wills," implying that North African people are less guided by their reason. Iago uses his own warped reasoning to convince Roderigo to continue in his passionate and ridiculous pursuit of Desdemona.

Shakespeare also poses the question: Has their passion for one another driven Othello and Desdemona to marry too soon? We hear of their wide age difference and their different cultural backgrounds. Desdemona admits that she knows of no signs of jealousy in Othello, whereas Othello readily believes his young wife can be unfaithful. His rational mind seems not to be working when he actually believes his wife has been with Cassio "a thousand times." How well do the two characters really know each other? Are they blinded by their passion?

Tying in with the theme of jealousy, Iago openly states that he wants to "put the Moor / At least into a jealousy so strong / That judgment cannot cure." Through his lies, Iago hopes that Othello's judgment will be unable to overcome his jealousy. Othello struggles with his strong and irrational feelings until his reason gives way to his misguided passion. When Desdemona finally realizes that Othello intends to murder her, she observes, "Some bloody passion shakes your very frame." Throughout the play she tries in vain to reason with her husband, but her words cannot overcome his passions.

# Motifs

Motifs are repeating elements in a narrative that take on a symbolic significance. Motifs often help reinforce the themes in a work and create a mood. As you'll see, many of the motifs in *Othello* help set the ominous tone of this tragic play.

## Monsters

Throughout *Othello*, Shakespeare repeatedly uses monster imagery to reinforce irrational and inhuman behavior. Is Iago simply a monster who destroys everything around him? Does Othello turn into a monster when his jealousy drives him to kill his innocent young wife? Through the recurring use of monster images, Shakespeare's play makes a case for the monster that may reside in even the purest heart.

At the end of his soliloquy in Act I, Scene 3, Iago describes his destructive plotting as a "monstrous birth" that he has brought into the world. His evil mind has given birth to a terrible idea that he will nurture and grow. While falsely counseling Othello not to become jealous, Iago refers to jealousy as "the green-eyed monster." When Iago describes Cassio's dream of having slept with Desdemona, Othello cries out in his anguish: "O monstrous! monstrous!"

Later in the play, Emilia describes jealousy as "a monster / Begot upon itself, born on itself." Desdemona responds, "Heaven keep that monster from Othello's mind!" Othello's description of his determination to kill Desdemona as a "strong conception" he groans with also plays on the birthing image. In this way Shakespeare ties together two motifs: the monster and the image of its birth, brought on by itself. These comments repeat Iago's original description of his evil plot as a birth.

Iago also plays on the fact that, in Elizabethan times, a man whose wife had been unfaithful was often called a "cuckold." Cuckolds were usually depicted as men with horns, another type of monster or devil. Othello refers to a cuckold as "a horned man ... a monster and a beast." In the final scene Emilia refers to Othello as "a devil" and Montano calls Othello's murder of Desdemona a "monstrous act."

This 1913 print by the artist Casavant shows the envy inspired by the "green-eyed monster" Shakespeare wrote about hundreds of years before.

### Kneeling

The motif of kneeling provides another of the play's most disturbing images. Although we never see a marriage scene between Othello and Desdemona, Othello kneels down with Iago at one point to take "a sacred vow." Kneeling beside Othello, Iago pledges his "wit, hands, heart / To wronged Othello's service." While they are kneeling in this scene that resembles a warped marriage vow, Othello asks Iago to kill Cassio. Othello then commits himself to murdering Desdemona.

Shakespeare repeats the image of kneeling when Desdemona kneels before Othello to ask him to clarify his accusations: "Upon my knees, what doth your speech import?" While kneeling, she pledges her allegiance to her husband as his "true and loyal wife." Desdemona later kneels again, this time before Iago, to ask for his help. "Here I kneel," she tells him as she professes her innocence to the very person who has been her undoing. The parallels to the earlier scene of Othello and Iago kneeling together are unmistakable.

## Symbols

Symbolism can take many forms in literature or in a play. These include physical objects, repeating words or phrases, characters, or even situations that represent something other than what they are on the surface. Just as a single bed on stage may represent an entire bedroom, symbols within the play itself suggest other meanings that help develop the central themes.

### The Handkerchief

In no other play by Shakespeare does an object carry as much symbolic weight as the handkerchief

By stealing Desdemona's handkerchief, Iago is able to destroy Othello's love for his wife.

in *Othello*. Throughout the play, it has a number of symbolic purposes. The handkerchief immediately functions as a symbol of early love between Othello and Desdemona. It is at first carelessly dropped by Othello when Desdemona offers him the handkerchief to bind his forehead because of a headache. He says he refuses it because it is "too little," and it falls unnoticed to the ground. We learn from Emilia, who finds it, that the handkerchief was Desdemona's "first remembrance"–her first gift–from Othello.

When Emilia gives the handkerchief to Iago, who has repeatedly asked her for it, the object becomes woven into his evil plan. Iago reveals he will intentionally "lose" the object in Cassio's lodgings, so that Cassio can find it there. Symbolically, Iago has transferred Desdemona's affection for Othello to Cassio.

Othello goes into a rage when Iago accurately describes the strawberry pattern on the handkerchief and says he saw Cassio wipe his beard with it. At this point in the play, the handkerchief becomes Othello's final proof, a symbol of Desdemona's infidelity (strawberries are shaped somewhat like hearts).

To Othello, the handkerchief also serves as a symbol of his heritage. When he confronts Desdemona about its location, he tells the story of its origin. We hear about the handkerchief's power to control affections between Othello's mother and father–and the danger of its loss. Losing it, Othello tells Desdemona, leads to disaster.

The handkerchief also comes to represent Othello's obsessive jealousy. He clings to the mistaken thought that his wife has given this token of his love and heritage to another man, Cassio. When he confronts Desdemona, he keeps repeating: "The handkerchief! ... The handkerchief!" Even in the final scene, when Desdemona denies having ever given it to Cassio, Othello accuses her of lying. Ultimately, the handkerchief becomes a symbol of truth when Emilia tells Othello that she gave it to Iago who had "begged" her to steal it. The former proof of his wife's unfaithfulness now becomes the proof of Iago's villainy.

## Life in Black and White

Shakespeare sets up a recurring contrast between black and white. Othello points out Desdemona's whiteness when he watches her sleeping before he smothers her to death. He says that her skin is "whiter ... than snow" and "smooth as ... alabaster." When Othello admits to Emilia that he has killed Desdemona, she responds: "O, the more angel she, / And you the blacker devil."

Although Othello refers to his own blackness ("I am black") at different points in the play, he also uses the color negatively to describe "black vengeance" when he hears about the handkerchief and is moved to rage.

Throughout *Othello*, Shakespeare uses the color black to represent evil and to reflect on Othello's place as a social outsider. Insults to Othello's race should not be confused with all uses of the color black. Although Othello is a North African, he receives only respect and admiration from the Venetian Senate, whose members side with him against Brabantio and support him as their military general. As the duke tells Brabantio: "Your son-in-law is far more fair than black." In this instance, the word "fair" implies true and virtuous, whereas the term "black"–though a pun on Othello's race–symbolizes a wicked or malevolent personality.

## Interpreting the Play

### Playing Othello—in Black and White

Discussions of race in *Othello* must be placed into historical context. As Britain became more involved in the slave trade in the seventeenth century, the image of a black hero proved increasingly problematic in productions. At times, white actors in England played Othello as a light-skinned Moor to avoid any potential offensiveness to white audiences. Many nineteenth-century scholars, including the Romantic poets Samuel Taylor Coleridge and Charles Lamb, argued about the validity of Othello's "blackness." Because these writers and directors were white in a time of segregated

# *A Game by Any Other Name*

YOU MAY HAVE played the popular board game called Othello, which requires flipping your opponent's discs until your color dominates the board. But this familiar game got its start under a different name: Reversi. It was invented by one of two Englishmen, Lewis Waterman or John W. Mollett. Each of the possible inventors accused the other of stealing their idea, and there is yet another (false) rumor that says the inventor was Goro Hasegawa of Japan. No matter the inventor responsible for the game, Shakespeare's famous quote from *Romeo and Juliet* seems appropriate: "A rose by any other name would smell as sweet." And it's probably true that Reversi is just as fun to play as Othello.

But the name change to Othello is no coincidence. Goro Hasegawa, who did not invent Reversi but *did* perfect the game into the one we know and love today, renamed the game after the famous Shakespearean play. The battle between black and white discs on the board mirrors the conflict between the Moor, Othello, and his white wife, Desdemona. The game is played on a green surface, which references both the battlefield that acts as the play's backdrop as well as the infamous color of jealousy–the motivation behind many of the characters' nefarious actions.

Even the game's strategy seems to reference the diabolical behavior of jealous Othello. Because of the game's early set up, with two white discs adjacent to two black discs, there is a situation

Originally called Reversi, the classic game of Othello was renamed after Shakespeare's woeful play about the struggle between good and evil.

at the end of the game called parity, where one can make large gains in a single move and secure their color by placing the last disc in a given section of the board.

The game Othello is just one of many places we can find Shakespeare's influence reach well beyond the theater's stage.

Orson Welles as Othello (1952)

societies, they could not accept the thought of a truly "black" Shakespearean hero.

In England, the tendency to play Othello as a white man (and, thus, by a white actor) was finally broken in 1930 when the African-American singer Paul Robeson played Othello in London. A black actor did not play Othello on stage in the Southern United States until 1979–and when he kissed Desdemona, audiences gasped and wrote hate letters.

Such revered African-American actors as James Earl Jones and Laurence Fishburne have lent their enormous talents to the role of Othello. With varying success, white actors such as Laurence Olivier and Orson Welles have played Othello in dark makeup. In 1997, the British-born actor Patrick Stewart played a white Othello in an all-black production, turning the play's racial imbalance on its head.

Contemporary playwrights have addressed the racial aspect from more political perspectives. For example, in Charles Marowitz's *An Othello* (1974), Iago is recast as a black radical questioning Othello's real motives. At the end of the play, Iago asks Othello: "Are you going to be a tool of white audiences just to give them a catharsis?" In *Harlem Duet* (1998), Canadian playwright Djanet Sears moves the action of Othello to Harlem in the nineteenth and twentieth centuries and focuses on the interracial marriage between Othello and Desdemona. Sears has referred to her play as "a rhapsodic blues tragedy."

## A Villain's Point of View

Shakespeare's inventive use of point of view in *Othello* brings the audience and reader closer to the events of this tragedy than to any other. By introducing us first to Iago and by immediately establishing Iago's hatred for Othello, Shakespeare creates a second layer of perspective that he adroitly maintains throughout the play. The establishment of Iago as the first and strongest voice in *Othello* also adds an element of irony to many of the play's events.

In *Othello*, it is the self-proclaimed villain who repeatedly takes us into his confidence. In this sense, Shakespeare cleverly brings us closest to Iago: we may sympathize with the other characters, but a part of us watches from Iago's viewpoint. Through Iago, Shakespeare appears to hold a mirror up to his audience. It may be easier to hate or feel disgust for Iago, but what part of ourselves do we see reflected in his odious behavior? This focused point of view brings us closer to the often-destructive consequences of feelings of envy and resentment.

Iago's words of intent regarding his plotting to destroy Othello keep us on the lookout for every character, event, or object that might feed into his malicious scheme. Therefore, Shakespeare adds a strong sense of dramatic irony to many events that seem innocuous. We cringe when Othello repeatedly calls Iago "honest," or when Cassio offers strong words of praise for Desdemona, or when a distraught Desdemona asks Iago for help. We know what the characters do not know: that Iago will use these good intentions to his own advantage, the essence of dramatic irony.

## Attitudes Toward Women in Othello

The male characters in *Othello* separate women into categories: either virginal idols (as Cassio worships "divine"

Desdemona and Emilia's strong roles in *Othello* would have been unusual in Shakespeare's day, yet their complexity keeps these characters relevant today.

Desdemona) or whores (represented by the frequent use of the word "strumpet"). Iago initiates this division in his satiric categorizing of women in Act II, Scene 1, when he accuses them of being duplicitous hussies who play various roles in society. Once Iago convinces Othello that Desdemona has been unfaithful, Othello assigns his wife the role of "strumpet." This misogyny (hatred of women) is emphasized in the scene in which Othello treats both Desdemona and Emilia as whores in a brothel. Before he kills Desdemona, Othello again calls her "strumpet!"–and Iago calls Emilia "villainous whore" before stabbing her to death.

Perceptions of the two main women in *Othello* have altered as attitudes toward women have changed. For centuries, the two women were played mostly as victims; at times, their roles were minimized and their lines deleted. Upon closer inspection, many of the lines Shakespeare wrote reveal two characters who often transcend the subordinate roles assigned to women in Elizabethan times.

Desdemona's loyalty to Othello and her love for her older husband drive her to remain faithful to him even as he becomes abusive. She tells Iago that Othello's "unkindness may defeat" her life but not her love. To modern audiences, this fealty may seem self-defeating and dangerous, though in Elizabethan times this proved Desdemona's purity of character.

As the action progresses, Emilia moves from playing Iago's dutiful wife to defying him and exposing her husband's deceit. In her conversation with Desdemona in Act IV, Scene 3, Emilia questions the double standard that allows for men's unfaithfulness and not women's. Her rhetorical questions concerning why men treat women as they do illustrate her main contention that wives have the same foibles as their husbands. In the final scene, Emilia's defiance of Iago and her bravery in telling the truth bring her character to the forefront of the action.

The significant roles given to these female characters challenge the legitimacy of the virgin/whore trope—a radical move in Shakespeare's day.

## A Play for All Time

It's amazing to think that a play written so long ago could maintain its resonance–yet that's what makes Shakespeare an enduring figure. Shakespeare's *Othello* holds a mirror to contemporary society and forces us to evaluate what we see reflecting back. All of Shakespeare's plays have this effect; they seem to evolve along with society. Each age relates to different themes in Shakespeare's multifaceted work. With any luck, perhaps readers of the future will relate less to Othello's issues of race, gender, and class. Perhaps instead they will relate to the characters, like Desdemona, who stand strong in their convictions.

# CHRONOLOGY

**1564** William Shakespeare is born on April 23 in Stratford-upon-Avon, England

**1578–1582** Span of Shakespeare's "Lost Years," covering the time between leaving school and marrying Anne Hathaway of Stratford

**1582** At age eighteen Shakespeare marries Anne Hathaway, age twenty-six, on November 28

**1583** Susanna Shakespeare, William and Anne's first child, is born in May, six months after the wedding

**1584** Birth of twins Hamnet and Judith Shakespeare

**1585–1592** Shakespeare leaves his family in Stratford to become an actor and playwright in a London theater company

**1587** Public beheading of Mary, Queen of Scots

**1593–94** The Bubonic (Black) Plague closes theaters in London

**1594–96** As a leading playwright, Shakespeare creates some of his most popular work, including *A Midsummer Night's Dream* and *Romeo and Juliet*

**1596** Hamnet Shakespeare dies in August at age eleven, possibly of plague

**1596–97** *The Merchant of Venice* and *Henry IV, Part One* most likely are written

**1599** The Globe Theatre opens

**1600** *Julius Caesar* is first performed at the Globe

**1600–01** *Hamlet* is believed to have been written

**1601–02** *Twelfth Night* is probably composed

**1603** Queen Elizabeth dies; Scottish king James VI succeeds her and becomes England's James I

**1604** Shakespeare pens *Othello*

**1605** *Macbeth* is composed

**1608–1610** London's theaters are forced to close when the plague returns and kills an estimated 33,000 people

**1611** *The Tempest* is written

**1613** The Globe Theater is destroyed by fire

**1614** Reopening of the Globe

**1616** Shakespeare dies on April 23

**1623** Anne Hathaway, Shakespeare's widow, dies; a collection of Shakespeare's plays, known as the First Folio, is published

# A SHAKESPEARE GLOSSARY

**addition** A name or title, such as knight, duke, duchess, king, etc.

**affect** To like or love; to be attracted to.

**approve** To prove or confirm.

**attend** To pay attention.

**belike** Probably.

**beseech** To beg or request.

**bondman** A slave.

**bootless** Futile; useless; in vain.

**broil** A battle.

**charge** Expense, responsibility; to command or accuse.

**common** A term describing the common people, below nobility.

**condition** Social rank; quality.

**countenance** Face; appearance; favor.

**cousin** A relative.

**curious** Careful; attentive to detail.

**discourse** To converse; conversation.

**discover** To reveal or uncover.

**dispatch** To speed or hurry; to send; to kill.

**doubt** To suspect.

**entreat** To beg or appeal.

**envy** To hate or resent; hatred; resentment.

**ere** Before.

**eyne** Eyes.

**fain** Gladly.

**fare** To eat; to prosper.

**favor** Face, privilege.

**fellow** A peer or equal.

**filial** Of a child toward its parent.

**fine** An end; "in fine" means in sum.

**folio** A book made up of individually printed sheets, each folded in half to make four pages; Shakespeare's folios contain all of his known plays in addition to other works.

**fond** Foolish.

**fool** A darling.

**genius** A good or evil spirit.

**gentle** Well-bred; not common.

**gentleman** One whose labor was done by servants. (Note: to call someone a gentleman was not a mere compliment on his manners; it meant that he was above the common people.)

**gentles** People of quality.

**get** To beget (a child).

**go to** "Go on"; "come off it."

**go we** Let us go.

**haply** Perhaps.

**happily** By chance; fortunately.

**hard by** Nearby.

**heavy** Sad or serious.

**husbandry** Thrift; economy.

**instant** Immediate.

**kind** One's nature; species.

**knave** A villain; a poor man.

**lady** A woman of high social rank. (Note: lady was not a synonym for woman or polite woman; it was not a compliment but simply a word referring to one's actual legal status in society, like gentleman.)

**leave** Permission; "take my leave" means depart (with permission).

**lief, lieve** "I had as lief" means I would just as soon; I would rather.

**like** To please; "it likes me not" means it is disagreeable to me.

**livery** The uniform of a nobleman's servants; emblem.

**Lord Chamberlain's Men** The company of players Shakespeare joined in London; under James I they became the King's Men.

**mark** Notice; pay attention.

**morrow** Morning.

**needs** Necessarily.

**nice** Too fussy or fastidious.

**owe** To own.

**passing** Very.

**peculiar** Individual; exclusive.

**privy** Private; secret.

**proper** Handsome; one's very own ("his proper son").

**protest** To insist or declare.

**quite** Completely.

**require** Request.

**several** Different, various.

**severally** Separately.

**sirrah** A term used to address social inferiors.

**sooth** Truth.

**state** Condition; social rank.

**still** Always; persistently.

**success** Result(s).

**surfeit** Fullness.

**touching** Concerning; about; as for.

**translate** To transform.

**unfold** To disclose.

**verse** Writing that uses a regular metrical rhythm and is divided from other lines by a space.

**villain** A low or evil person; originally, a peasant.

**voice** A vote; consent; approval.

**vouchsafe** To confide or grant.

**vulgar** Common.

**want** To lack.

**weeds** Clothing.

**what ho** "Hello, there!"

**wherefore** Why.

**wit** Intelligence; sanity.

**withal** Moreover; nevertheless.

**without** Outside.

**would** Wish.

# SUGGESTED ESSAY TOPICS

1. Using references and examples from the play, argue for or against this statement: Othello is responsible for his own downfall and the loss of everything that matters to him. Remember to develop a strong thesis statement.

2. Discuss the role that social class plays in *Othello*. How do economics and social standing affect both character behavior and events throughout the play? What effect does social class have on the tragedy that takes place?

3. Discuss the state of race relations in the context of the play. How does race affect both Othello's view of himself and the other characters' views of Othello? Does our modern worldview alter the play's racial aspects?

4. Watch one of the DVDs of *Othello* and write an essay comparing and contrasting the director's interpretation and Shakespeare's play. In light of having read the play closely, discuss what is or is not successful about the performance, including what the director has changed and the actors playing the roles.

5. In a well-developed essay, respond to Emilia's speech in Act IV, Scene 3, about women and men. Emilia claims, "I do think it is their husbands' faults / If wives do fail." Explain and respond to her various arguments throughout her speech to Desdemona.

# TEST YOUR MEMORY

1. The military rank Iago feels has been stolen from him is:
   a) ensign; b) general; c) captain; d) lieutenant.

2. The play's action takes place in two places, Venice and:
   a) Verona; b) Cyprus; c) Ceylon; d) London.

3. As a Moor, Othello originally comes from:
   a) North Africa b) Southeast Asia; c) India; d) South America.

4. Brabantio is Desdemona's:
   a) father; b) uncle; c) servant; d) clown.

5. The Venetians have been warring with these people:
   a) the Africans; b) the Turks; c) the Florentines; d) the British.

6. This character is accused of using black magic:
   a) Othello; b) Brabantio; c) Iago; d) Desdemona.

7. This lovelorn character wants to drown himself:
   a) Cassio; b) Othello; c) Roderigo; d) Iago.

8. This character has a problem with drinking alcohol:
   a) Cassio; b) Roderigo; c) Othello; d) Clown.

9. This character cries out: "I have lost my reputation!": a) Cassio; b) Othello; c) Roderigo; d) Iago.

10. Cassio bribes this character:
a) Roderigo; b) Emilia; c) Iago; d) Clown.

11. The person who calls jealousy a "green-eyed monster" is: a) Emilia; b) Iago; c) Othello; d) Desdemona.

12. This character says about Desdemona: "She did deceive her father, marrying you": a) Iago; b) Brabantio; c) Roderigo; d) Lodovico.

13. Othello believes Desdemona has been unfaithful with this man:
a) Iago; b) Roderigo; c) Gratiano; d) Cassio.

14. This character finds the handkerchief on the ground: a) Bianca ; b) Desdemona ; c) Emilia ; d) Othello.

15. The pattern on the handkerchief features these objects: a) hearts ; b) tears ; c) ships ; d) strawberries.

16. Bianca is:
a) Desdemona's servant; b) Cassio's wife; c) Iago's mistress; d) a courtesan.

17. He asks Bianca to make a copy of the handkerchief: a) Othello; b) Cassio; c) Iago; d) Roderigo.

18. He stabs and kills Roderigo:
a) Cassio; b) Montano; c) Iago; d) Othello.

**19.** At the end of the play, Iago is:
a) killed by Lodovico; b) killed by Othello; c) wounded by Lodovico; d) wounded by Othello.

**20.** At the end of the play, Othello:
a) is imprisoned; b) is stabbed by Iago; c) is killed by Lodovico; d) stabs himself and dies.

## Answer Key

1: D, 2: B, 3: A, 4: A, 5: B, 6: A, 7: C, 8: A, 9: A, 10: D, 11: B, 12: A, 13: D, 14: C, 15: D, 16: D, 17: B, 18: C, 19: D, 20: D.

# FURTHER INFORMATION

## Books


Goodwin, Vincent, and William Shakespeare. *William Shakespeare's Othello* (Graphic Shakespeare). Edina, MN: Magic Wagon, 2009.

Shakespeare, William, and Jason Scott. *Othello: Side by Side.* Cheswold, DE: Prestwick House, 2005.

Shakespeare, William, and Kim F. Hall. *Othello, the Moor of Venice: Texts and Contexts.* Boston: Bedford/St. Martin's, 2007.


## Websites

### The Folger Shakespeare Library

http://www.folger.edu/othello

Navigate the Folger Library's digital image repository, where some of the earliest photographs of actors portraying Othello have been archived.

### The Royal Shakespeare Company

http://www.rsc.org.uk/othello

Learn more about past stagings of *Othello* and the history of the play. The Royal Shakespeare Company's website also provides a roundup of links to other *Othello* sites.

## Shakespeare Online

http://www.shakespeare-online.com/playanalysis/othello.html

Explore character descriptions, quotations, and the "stage history" of *Othello*.

## Films

*"O."* Directed by Tim Blake Nelson, starring Mekhi Phifer, Josh Hartnett, and Julia Stiles, 2001.

*Othello*. Directed by Oliver Parker, starring Laurence Fishburne and Kenneth Branagh, 2000.

*Othello*. Directed by Stuart Burge and John Dexter, starring Laurence Olivier and Maggie Smith, 1965.

# BIBLIOGRAPHY


Bentley, Gerald Eades. "*Othello, the Moor of Venice.*" William Shakespeare: The Compete Works. Edited by Alfred Harbage. Baltimore: Penguin Books, 1969.

Bloom, Harold. *Shakespeare's Othello*. New York: Riverhead Trade, 2005.

Bradley, A. C. *Shakespearean Tragedy: Lectures on Hamlet, Othello, King Lear and Macbeth*. New York: Palgrave Macmillan, 2007.

Bryson, Bill. *Shakespeare: The World as Stage*. New York: HarperCollins, 2007.

Harbage, Alfred. *A Reader's Guide to Shakespeare*. New York: Farrar, Straus and Giroux, 1974.

Holste, Gayle, ed. *Othello*. Shakespeare Made Easy. Hauppauge, NY: Barron's, 2002.

Honigmann, E.A.J., Ed. *Othello*. The Arden Shakespeare. London: Arden, 2006.

Neill, Michael. Introduction to *The Oxford Shakespeare: Othello*. Oxford World's Classics. Edited by Stanley Wells. Oxford and New York: Oxford University Press, 2006.

Milward, Peter, *Shakespeare's Meta-Drama: Othello and King Lear*. Tokyo, Japan: Renaissance Institute/Sophia University, 2003.

Pearce, Joseph. *The Quest for Shakespeare: The Bard of Avon and the Church of Rome*. San Francisco: Ignatius Press, 2008.

Pechter, Edward. *Othello and Interpretive Traditions.* Iowa City: University of Iowa Press, 1999.

Shakespeare, William. *The Oxford Shakespeare Othello.* Edited by Michael Neill. Oxford World's Classics. Edited by Stanley Wells. Oxford and New York: Oxford University Press, 2006.

# INDEX

# ABOUT THE AUTHORS

**Edith Jones** has a master's degree in British Literature that she puts to good use teaching high school and college students. She has written extensively about the influence of William Shakespeare. In her spare time, Jones enjoys reading, running marathons, and memorizing sonnets.

**Tatiana Ryckman** is a writer, editor, and teacher. She holds a bachelor's degree in journalism and a master's degree in creative writing. Other books by Ryckman for Cavendish Square include a biography of Oprah Winfrey called *Oprah Winfrey: Media Mogul and Philanthropist*; and a biography of Alexander Hamilton, called *Alexander Hamilton: The First Secretary of Treasury and an Author of the Federalist Papers*. When she is not writing, she enjoys reading and bicycling with friends in Austin, Texas.